E-Learning Uncovered:

From Concept to Execution

Desirée Ward
Diane Elkins

ALCORN WARD
& Partners, Inc.

E-Learning Uncovered: From Concept to Execution

By Desirée Ward and Diane Elkins

Copyright © 2009 by Alcorn, Ward, & Partners, Inc.

Alcorn, Ward, & Partners, Inc.

2771-29 Monument Road #329

Jacksonville, FL 32225

www.alcorn-ward.com

Trademarks

Lectora is a registered trademarks of Trivantis Corporation. Microsoft and PowerPoint are registered trademarks of Microsoft Corporation. Captivate and Flash are registered trademarks of Adobe Systems Incorporated.

Other product and company names mentioned herein may be the trademarks of their respective owners. Use of trademarks or product names is not intended to convey endorsement or affiliation with this book.

Warning and Disclaimer

The information provided is on an "as is" basis. Every effort has been made to make this book as complete and as accurate as possible, but no warranty or fitness is imlied. The authors and the publisher shall have neither liability or responsibility to any person or entity with respect to any loss or damages arising from the information contained in this book.

Table of Contents
Overview

Table of Contents
Details

Chapter 1

Chapter 2

Chapter 3

Table of Contents

Chapter 4

Table of Contents

Chapter 5

Chapter 6

Chapter 7

Table of Contents

Chapter 8

Chapter 9

Chapter 10

Chapter 11

Chapter 12

Table of Contents

What Is e-Learning?

From the day we were born, we have been learners who actively take in information from the world around us – in both formal and informal ways. Before a child says his first word, the parent doesn't have a structured outline with ways to meet specific objectives – it is done informally. On the other hand, much of our childhood education comes from a very structured environment with objectives, lessons, assignments, and tests.

Now we use electronic medium such as computers, CDs, and the Internet for informal and formal learning. So, what is e-learning? It is any learning that occurs with the assistance of an electronic medium.

If you have ever learned anything from a Website, if you have ever posted a question on a discussion forum and gotten an answer, or if you have ever looked up a computer tip through the software's help feature: you have experienced e-learning in the informal sense of the word.

In a more formal sense (and for the purposes of this book), e-learning is any course or structured learning event that uses an electronic medium to meet its objectives. It can have many of the same elements of the more traditional learning (text, audio, tests, homework, etc.), but uses a computer to meet or enhance the learning objectives.

The pages and chapters that follow will give you everything you need to know to decide if a concept will be suitable for e-learning and, if so, how to take that concept to a fully executed course.

Types of e-Learning

e-Learning can be divided into three main types. These types are based on the timing of the course and involvement with others. Selecting the appropriate method involves considering the learner's prior knowledge, learning speed, time available, and geographic separation. The three main types of e-learning are:

- Synchronous Learning
- Asynchronous Learning
- Virtual Classroom Learning

While synchronous and virtual classroom techniques and strategies will be addressed in this book, the main focus will be asynchronous learning.

Synchronous Learning

Synchronous learning occurs when an instructor and students are together at the same time – but not necessarily in the same physical place.

Traditional classroom learning is a great example of synchronous learning. During a traditional classroom session, students meet at a set time, have discussions, and are tested together.

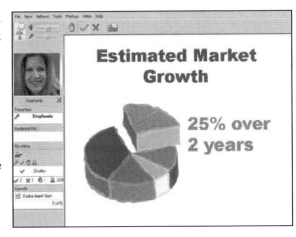

A synchronous e-learning course uses the same concept. At a set period of time, an instructor and one or more students participate in an electronic learning event. Examples include a Web broadcast (Webcast), Web seminar (Webinar), or meetings in a virtual world, such as **Second Life**.

Asynchronous Learning

Asynchronous learning is the opposite of synchronous learning. It occurs when the instructor and students do not participate at the same time or when there is no instructor at all.

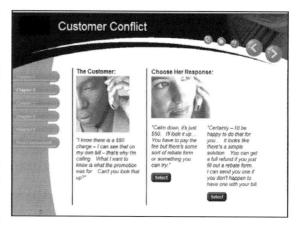

In the world of traditional education, think of homework as asynchronous learning. If students are given an activity to complete on their own time by themselves, the learning is asynchronous.

In the world of e-learning, a self-paced course that can be accessed at any time and does not require the involvement of an instructor or peers would be considered asynchronous.

Virtual Classroom Learning

The virtual classroom combines elements of the synchronous and asynchronous world. There are students and an instructor as well as a specified beginning and end date. However, within the course, students learn and communicate on their own time.

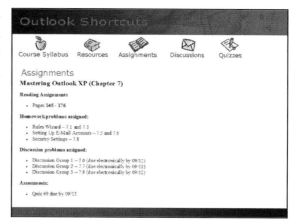

For example, in a synchronous leadership Webinar, everyone would log onto their computers at 2:00 on Tuesday and participate in the presentation until it was over at 4:00. In a virtual classroom, the students might log on in the first week of the month, but could then read the materials, complete the activities, and discuss issues with other classmates at any time during the month.

Many colleges and universities are using such virtual classrooms as **Blackboard** for online classes that are allowing students to take classes without going to the colleges' locations. The virtual classroom allows students to interact through the use of on-line forums and discussion boards and allows knowledge sharing with documents posted for others to view.

Alphabet Soup: e-Learning Acronyms

CBT *(Computer-Based Training):* *Any e-learning course designed to be either housed on the World Wide Web, an intranet, or a computer disc (CD).*

WBT *(Web-Based Training):* *An e-learning course that is designed to be housed on the World Wide Web and taken while you are connected to the Internet.*

Other variations with similar meanings:

> *CAL: Computer-Assisted Learning*

> *CMI: Computer-Managed Instruction*

> *TBT: Technology-Based Training*

Blended Learning

Blended learning uses two or more learning formats to help meet your objectives. For example, you may develop asynchronous e-learning modules to present factual information, and then invite the student to participate in classroom instruction where they can have face-to-face discussions or hands-on practice.

Advantages and Disadvantages of e-Learning

There is rarely a decision that has to be made in life that doesn't have advantages and disadvantages for both sides. The same is true for what learning platform you choose for your course. It is important to weigh the advantages and disadvantages of the possibilities before you make a final decision.

What is best – traditional classroom learning or e-learning? Or, is a blended solution best? Take a look at the advantages and disadvantages of e-learning so you can decide for yourself.

Advantages of e-Learning

Viewed Anywhere

e-Learning programs can be viewed anywhere in the world where a computer is available. You can choose to present your course in the following 4 formats:

- Disk – Generally a course will fit on a compact disk (CD). Or for courses with large media files, you may choose to put it on a digital video disk (DVD). The advantages to having your course on a disk is that it is portable, does not take up space on your hard drive, and the computer does not need an Internet connection.

- Computer – The course could be permanently placed on your computer's hard drive. Though this takes up memory, it could be more convenient than carrying a CD or having to connect to a network.

- Internet – Your course could be housed on the Internet. This convenient method allows for quick changes to the course, does not take up valuable space on your hard drive, and does not require that your computer have a CD drive to be able to view it.

- Intranet – Your course could be placed on an internal company network that can only be accessed by employees of the company. This increases security, but sometimes makes it more difficult for remote employees to access the courses.

- Mobile Device – Your course could be viewed on a mobile device such as a cellular phone or personal desktop assistant (PDA). Depending on the mobile device being used, the course could be downloaded to the device, placed on the Internet, or it could use cellular lines to get course.

Used Anytime

Because of time zone differences and people's busy schedules, it is valuable to have a solution that allows students to learn when they can fit it into their schedule. If learners want to view an online course during lunch, during a regular work day, or at 3:00 in the morning – they can!

Less Expensive for Many Users

e-Learning is an expensive solution if only a few people will be learning from it. If, however, many people will be taking the course, it could cost significantly less than the traditional classroom model. For example, if a trainer is required in locations throughout the world, you could save on travel and lodging costs with an e-learning program.

Tracking Capabilities

An e-learning course can be set up to track such things as who took a course, how long a person spent reviewing the course materials, how well he or she did on tests. This can be very valuable information, especially for mandatory or certification classes that require proof of completion.

Self-Paced Learning

Learning speed can vary greatly from person to person. e-Learning courses allow people to study at their own pace. Slower learners can feel free to take their time learning information and faster learners can go through the materials at a quicker pace and still get the information they need from the course.

Review Tool

Once material has been learned, it is possible for students to go back and review areas that they don't remember or that they need some pointers for. This is very useful when there are concepts or procedures that aren't used often or are very complex.

Knowledge Base for Just-In-Time Learning

Sometimes employees do not need a full course – they just need a little bit of information to help them with what they are doing at the moment. e-Learning can help meet the immediate need for training. Examples of just-in-time training include a help menu in a computer program or an online checklist to prepare for an interview.

Delivered Immediately

Well, the course may not be *ready* immediately. But once a course has been developed and posted, employees can take it as soon as they need it – rather than waiting until the next time the course is offered.

Unlimited Simultaneous Users

Where classroom courses can only allow a certain amount of learners per session, an e-learning course can be available to unlimited users at any given time. This can allow many people in multiple locations to get access to valuable information right away. This is useful when the entire company needs time-sensitive information and you don't want to wait for the trainers to be able to get to all locations.

Disadvantages of e-Learning

While e-learning can solve some of the problems of classroom learning, there can be disadvantages for using it to meet some objectives and for some courses.

Cost

While an e-learning program may end up being cheaper per user, it isn't cheap! Between development costs, hardware and software, and ongoing maintenance, you could spend anywhere from a few thousand to over a million dollars. If you have a small audience or budget, e-learning may not make sense for you. You can find out more about the costs of e-learning in Chapter 3.

Collaboration

Some of the best learning in a classroom often comes from the interaction with the instructor and other students. While this collaboration is not impossible with e-learning, there will probably not be as much of it.

Technology

If the right technology is not in place, can't be afforded, and/or can't be supported, e-learning can be frustrating or even futile. Anyone who has tried to watch a video on a dial-up Internet connection knows this.

Computer Literacy

Some learners may not be able to use a computer. If your students have never used a computer before, they may not be able to figure out how to turn it on, let alone be able to complete an e-learning course. It is important to know your audience and make concessions for training the learners first on how to use the needed technology.

Computer Availability

Not everybody has access to a computer. If you do not supply computers to all employees in your organization, it could be difficult for some to take e-learning courses.

Computer Compatibility

Not all courses can be used with all types of computers and operating systems. It is important to know what your audience has and decide if your course can be viewed by everybody in your target audience.

Unanswered Questions

With many e-learning courses, it is difficult for the students to find answers to any questions that are left unanswered after they have completed the course. The goal with developing e-learning is to answer the questions before they are asked.

Energy and Excitement

Classroom sessions can be used to generate excitement and get buy-in about a particular subject. In addition, a classroom session might be a refreshing break away from a production line or cubicle. Learning online does not tend to create the same kind of excitement and energy.

Elements of an e-Learning Course

e-Learning courses can take many shapes and sizes. However, there are certain elements that are common among most courses. Starting out with an understanding of these elements will help as we move soon to discussions on planning and analysis. Each of the elements listed here is explained with more detail in chapters 6 and 7.

Interface

The interface is the visual framework for each screen. It includes the overall course graphics and shows the buttons, features, and navigation that will be used throughout the course. Think of it as the elements that are the same on every screen.

Text

In an asynchronous course, when audio isn't being used, the majority of the content could be delivered via on-screen text. The text can be displayed in the text area of the interface, but can also be part of the interactions.

This is what makes an e-learning course without audio different than a PowerPoint presentation that accompanies a classroom training session. The PowerPoint uses text to highlight important points, but does not provide all the content. Where the instructor provides the details of the content in the classroom, the text in an e-learning course has to provide all the details you want to communicate.

Navigation

The navigation for a course allows the learner to move through the course. Navigation buttons such as arrows, hyperlinks, and menus can all help the student move through the course. Navigation can be fixed (where the student has to proceed in a linear fashion from the beginning to the end) or flexible (where the student can choose where to go).

Interactions

Interactions are any events or activities that requires the student to respond in some way. Examples include a spot that the student clicks to get additional information, a question the student must answer, or a practice simulation.

Interactions keep the learner interested and enhance the learning experience. They are often the most interesting part of the e-learning course. However, they can also be the most expensive.

Tests

The ability to administer a test is a very popular feature in e-learning. Tests questions can use several formats:

- Multiple Choice
- Drag and Drop
- True/False
- Fill in the Blank
- Short Answer
- Essay
- Simulations

Some of these question formats require an instructor to provide feedback, while some can be graded directly in the course. Tests can be used at the beginning of a course, at the end of a course, at the end of individual modules, or even scattered throughout the course.

Media

Technically, an e-learning course could consist only of on-screen text. But a more engaging course would use a number of different media elements, such as:

- <u>Audio</u> – Audio can be used in place of on-screen text to deliver the primary content, in conjunction with the on-screen text (used as straight narration), or used in individual situations such as a role-play or scenario.

- <u>Video</u> – Like audio, video can be used as the primary method of content delivery or to provide additional information for specific teaching points.

- <u>Graphics</u> – Graphics include any still photography, clip-art pictures, graphs, or diagrams that are included in your course. They can be informational or decorative in nature.

- <u>Animations</u> – Animations are moving graphics. For example, if you are creating a course about a manufacturing process, you could create a moving graphic that simulates the flow through the different production departments.

Collaboration

Collaboration is the activity of learners working together to reach a learning goal. In the classroom, collaboration occurs anytime one student turns to another and makes a comment, asks a question, or works with someone on a project. In e-learning this can occur in forums, blogs, shared documents, and wikis.

Forum

A forum is a collaborative learning experience where questions or comments are posted and a trail of responses are posted and archived regarding the original message. Often called threaded discussions or message boards, forums are asynchronous forms of communication and message sending.

Blog

A blog, short for web log, is a type of Website where someone writes short entries on a regular basis, much like a column in a newspaper. Readers can then leave comments. Some blogs are written by a single person, while others have shared writing responsibilities among several people. A typical blog combines text, images, and links to other Web pages with information on a topic.

Shared Documents

Documents can be stored on a shared server such as an intranet or SharePoint site for collaborative authoring and editing. People can check out documents and add content, make changes, and comment on the information.

Wiki

A wiki is a type of Website that uses a special software allowing easy creation and editing of interlinked Web pages. With wikis, users are invited to edit any page or create a new page within the wiki Web site – involving the user in an ongoing process of creation and collaboration that constantly changes the knowledge base. **Wikipedia**, the collaborative encyclopedia, is one of the best-known wikis.

Tracking

One of the main reasons companies choose to use e-learning is the ability to track progress, completion, and test scores. If set up to do so, e-learning courses can send this information to be tracked. In the simplest forms, the information might be sent via an e-mail. In more formal situations, the information will be fed to a Learning Management System (LMS) that will compile and store the information. Especially when a course is mandatory per regulation, it is important to be able to prove a learner did take and pass the course.

Summary

e-Learning uses an electronic medium to allow learners to learn collaboratively or on their own; at their own pace or at the pace of a group. It has multiple advantages, as well as disadvantages in comparison to other platforms. So, it's important to weigh the options and decide what is best for your particular course and objectives.

Future chapters will help you determine how the advantages and disadvantages apply to your environment, how to select the right format, and the best way to include the different course elements.

2

Developing an e-Learning Strategy

"Everybody is doing it."

"I've heard it will save us money."

"My bonus is tied to it."

"The CEO read an article about it and now we have to deliver 50% of our training online by the end of the year."

e-Learning projects have been started (and have occasionally been successful) with very little thought or justification. However, most projects will benefit from thoughtful consideration as to the whys and the hows before jumping right in.

This chapter will help you identify the questions you need to ask and the process you might want to follow to determine if e-learning is a good solution, the best way to approach it, and how to get everyone on board.

Strategic Plans and e-Learning

Many different models, outlines, templates, and checklists exist that provide guidance on how to conduct strategic planning for any issue. Some are elaborate; some are simple, but they all contain the basics.

- What are you trying to do?
- Why are you trying to do it?
- How are you going to get there?

While this is an extremely simplistic model, it is amazing how many projects get started without looking at these questions even at a high level.

Benefits of a Strategic Plan

A good strategic plan can take a lot of time and effort to develop, but it can serve many purposes as well. It can help you:

- Decide if you even want to embark on an e-learning journey.
- Generate support from key stakeholders.
- Request funding from internal or external sources.
- Reach consensus on what it will take to make the project happen.
- Notify everyone of potential risks and challenges.
- Ensure you are doing this for the right reasons.
- Create a common picture of what success would look like.
- Point you in the right direction for getting started.

In the end, any of the platitudes about proper planning (such as, "if you fail to plan, you plan to fail" and "begin with the end in mind") apply to an e-learning project. The strategic plan gets you started.

How Detailed Should a Strategic Plan Be?

Only you and the people making the decisions about your project can answer this question. And the real answer may come in phases. For example, you may want to develop an extremely high-level cost-benefit analysis just to decide if it is worth the time and effort needed to build a more detailed business case. Then, when you are ready to ask for the funding and support, you may need a more detailed plan.

Strategic Plans vs. Business Cases

Some organizations use these terms interchangeably. Generally, the business case is a subset of a strategic plan. A business case generally addresses the "What?" and the "Why?" questions. A strategic plan also addresses the "How?"

Strategic Plans vs. Project Plans

The "How?" portion of a strategic plan can overlap with the project plan. So how do you know where to draw the line? The strategic plan includes enough detail to ensure everyone knows what you are trying to accomplish and what it will take to make it happen. Your project plan will include all the detail to actually make it happen.

Consider the difference between a travel guide and a travel map. A travel guide will help you determine where you will go, what you will see, and help you map out a general itinerary. That's your strategic plan. But when it comes time to actually go on the trip, you will need a road map to help decide which interstate and which exit to use. That's your project plan.

Possible Elements in a Strategic Plan

Select the elements that relate to your decision-making process.

Executive Summary

Problem Statement

Background

Project Objectives

Proposed Solution

Cost/Benefit Analysis

Alternative Solutions

Recommendation

Deliverables

Quality Criteria

Resource Requirements

Known Constraints

Estimated Timeline

Proposed Budget

Critical Success Factors

Implementation Plan

Evaluation Plan

Management Plan

Risks

Risk Management Plan

The Underlying Business Goals and Benefits

The foundation of any business strategy is: WHY? In this case, why do you want e-learning?

In the previous chapter, you learned about the advantages and disadvantages of e-learning. Now it is time to take those advantages and tie them to the issues and drivers in your organization. A training professional might first jump to the learning or training management benefits of e-learning, but it is best to start a few levels higher – with the business benefits.

Know What You Are Analyzing

When building the business case and reviewing the cost/benefit analysis, make sure you understand exactly WHAT you are evaluating.

- Are you comparing an e-learning course to no training at all?

- Are you comparing an e-learning course to the same course delivered in another format?

- Are you examining the benefits of computer-based training and learning management?

The answers to these questions will determine which parts of the analysis process you will use. For example, if you are looking to convert an existing training course to e-learning, should you include the benefits for conducting the training itself, or just the benefits for using the new format? If you are considering the use of online courses as well as a learning management system, should you separate out the business cases, or treat them as one?

Decide in advance exactly what decisions you and your company need to make and exactly what benefits and numbers will best help you make those decisions.

Tying e-Learning to Business Goals

To identify how e-learning ties into the organization's overall goals, ask yourself (and key stakeholders) the following questions:

- What business problems are we trying to solve?
- What business problems are we trying to prevent?
- What strategic goals does the company have that e-learning would support?
- What strategic goals does the company have that e-learning might hinder?

You will be in a better position to generate support and funding if you can show how the e-learning initiative is tied to the overall company strategy.

Benefits of the Training Program

If you are proposing a brand new training program, you will want to analyze the benefits of conducting the program. This process is the same whether you are looking at classroom delivery or online delivery. Using a combination of interviews, brainstorming, and statistics, you'll want to create a list of anticipated benefits that include things like:

- Time saved
- Productivity increased
- Service increased
- Turnover reduced
- Quality increased
- Safety violations reduced
- Sales increased
- Money saved
- Liability decreased

And any other factors related to the project you are reviewing.

Benefits of the e-Learning Delivery Platform

Sometimes an e-learning project is not about the content – it is about the delivery method. Perhaps you have an effective classroom training program in place, but the question on the table is, "What are the business benefits for converting to a different delivery platform?"

Use the checklist in Figure 2.1 to see if you have some of the environmental factors that often make e-learning a good fit.

For any question where you answered "yes," determine the benefits to you for using e-learning to deal with that issue. For example:

- If you have a geographically-dispersed workforce, you might benefit from reduced travel costs, from providing training to smaller locations that currently don't receive the same training as the large offices, and from a consistent training message to all employees.

- If you have a wide variety of pre-existing knowledge on a subject, you might benefit from less time spent in training overall if the experienced employees can skip the sections they already understand or can at least cover them at a quicker pace; or you could benefit from increased understanding by your inexperienced employees because they can take as much time as they need to really understand.

Continue through all items that apply to you until you have uncovered all the benefits you can think of.

Benefits of a Training Management System

If you are considering the use of a Learning Management System (LMS), Learning Content Management System (LCMS), or other administrative software, continue the process by identifying the benefits of such a system. Benefits might include:

- Reduced data entry time
- Increased protection against liability
- Reduced time needed to create compliance documentation
- Increased training completion due to automated registrations, reminders, and exception reports

You can read more about training management systems in chapter 4.

Figure 2.1 Do You Need e-Learning? Quiz

Go to the Resources page at **www.e-LearningUncovered.com** for a printable version of this quiz.

	Yes	Some	No
1. Do you have a geographically-dispersed workforce?			
2. Does your audience work in different time zones or on different shifts?			
3. Do you have to train on a subject frequently?			
4. Do you have people with low productivity or high error rates because they have to wait for the next training class to be offered?			
5. Do you have a large number of people to train?			
6. Do you have mandated training?			
7. Do you need to reach a lot of people very quickly (such as product knowledge for a new launch or a new legal requirement)?			
8. Do you need to train on complex information?			
9. Would it be useful for people to be able to go back and study a section again?			
10. Do you have a wide variety of pre-existing knowledge on a subject (some are learners are experienced, some are novices, and some in the middle)?			
11. Do different portions of your audience need slightly different information?			
12. Would you like people to be able to test out?			
13. Would your information benefit from video or animation (such as a moving diagram of how a manufacturing process works)?			
14. Would you like to provide the same level of training in less time?			

NOTE: There is no scoring for this quiz. If you say yes to just one question, and it's a big enough issue for you, then that alone may justify an e-learning project. Conversely, you may say yes to five or six questions, but another factor might make e-learning inappropriate. Use this to help you understand the business drivers.

Cost/Benefit Analysis

The core of your business case will be the cost/benefit analysis. This can be a formal, quantitative analysis including a complete ROI statement, or an informal, qualitative approach that considers tangible as well as intangible benefits.

This section will focus on the cost/benefit analysis and return on investment estimates for the use of an e-learning delivery platform. If you want to conduct a similar assessment on the need for a particular training program, there are many excellent resources available to help you. For now, assume the training need has been justified, and the use of an e-learning delivery platform is what is being considered.

Quantifying Benefits

Perhaps the hardest part of building a business case is trying to quantify the impact of all the benefits you just identified. Some might be easy to quantify, such as reduced travel costs. Some may be almost impossible to quantify, such as increased morale. Most, however, fall somewhere in between.

Most benefits can be quantified by asking two questions:

- To what degree?
- At what cost/savings?

These factors, when combined with the number of people affected, can give you a numerical value for the benefit.

Coming up with the answers to the two core questions may be challenging. Look to other departments to see if they already have metrics around some of the issues. For example, does the Human Resources department know your current turnover rate as well as the cost to hire a new employee? Does the production department have numbers about the error rates of new employees versus those who have completed training? Does the customer service department know the cost of a dropped call?

An Example

Consider that using the e-learning platform will reduce the amount of time your sales people will be away from time actually selling.

• To what degree? How much more time will they be able to sell?

• At what cost or savings? If a salesperson is selling 5 hours a month more, how much is that likely to increase sales?

Through research and interviews, you determine that 5 hours a month increased sales activity is likely to lead to .5 more sales per month with a company average order of $6,000. There are 35 sales reps.

Monthly benefit = .5 x 6,000 x 35 = $105,000 increased sales per month

Most likely you will come up with some benefits that you just cannot quantify. You will have to decide, then, how you want to deal with them. Some organizations choose not to include them if they cannot be quantified. Others create a separate section that deals with "intangibles."

Quantifying Costs

To determine if the benefits are worth it, you will want to create a high-level estimate for the overall cost of the program.

Direct Program Costs

This can be challenging early on in an e-learning project because you haven't yet made a lot of the decisions that will go into your ultimate project budget. At this point, you will want to come up with some estimated high-level numbers about what you will need to spend. Refer to Chapter 3 for help in determining your direct program costs.

Indirect Costs

In addition to the direct costs, you will also want to determine if there are any indirect costs. The most common indirect cost for a training program would be an opportunity cost – what could your money and people be doing if they weren't doing this, and what is the cost of that missed opportunity?

So in this case, what would your training team, your SMEs, or your IT team be doing if they were not working on this project?

Comparison Methods

Once you have identified and quantified your costs and benefits, you can evaluate the business case.

Comparing Costs to Costs

If you are looking at converting an existing classroom program to an online delivery format, you would simply compare the cost of each in a side-by-side comparison. To do this, you will want to estimate the shelf life of the materials and project the costs out for that period of time.

Figure 2.2 Sample Cost Comparison for Six-Hour Orientation Program

Classroom Delivery			Online Delivery	
Costs for 1 class of 15 per month			*Costs for 3-hour online course*	
Materials	$5,400		Contract Development	$45,000
Instructor's Salary	$6,480		Student Wages @ $10/hr	$16,200
Refreshments	$5,940			
Student Wages @ $10/hr	$32,400			
Total Cost for 3 years	$50,220		Total Cost for 3 years	$61,200

Figure 2.3 Sample Cost Comparison for New Product Training (including intangibles)

Classroom Delivery		Online Delivery	
Costs for 35 people for 1 day class		*Costs for 3-hour online course*	
Contract Development	$8,000	Contract Development	$45,000
Materials	$350	Materials (CD, etc.)	$175
Instructor's Salary	$500	Lost sales while in training (Training taken during non-productive times such as flights or while waiting for meetings)	$0
Facilities	$750		
Refreshments	$450		
Travel (mileage)	$850		
Lodging (for 4 reps)	$300	10% reduced sales of new product for first 2 months because opportunity for practice was not provided.	$71,400
Lost sales while in training and transit	$210,000		
Total Cost	$221,200	Total Cost	$116,575

Comparing Costs to Benefits

Rather than comparing the two sets of costs, you could simply look at the costs vs. the benefits of the one delivery option.

Figure 2.4 Costs vs. Benefits for a Learning Management System

Benefits over 3 years		Costs over 3 years	
Elimination of 1.5 FTE Training Assistants	$189,000	Hardware upgrades	$12,000
		Software License	$35,000
		Implementation & Testing	$15,000
		.25 FTE LMS Administrator	$67,500
Total Cost for 3 years	$189,000	Total Cost for 3 years	$129,500

Calculation Methods

There are a number of different ways you can present your bottom line numbers. Cost-Benefit Ratio and Return on Investment are two of the most common.

Cost Benefit Ratio

Financial Benefits ÷ Total Cost of Training = Cost-Benefit Ratio

Example: $189,000 ÷ $129,500 = 1.46

This means that for every dollar invested, it will return $1.46.

Different organizations have different opinions about what an acceptable cost-benefit ratio is. Some would say that anything over the break-even point (1.0) is worth doing since that is the break-even point. Some would say that there is not enough benefit to be worth the trouble unless the benefit is a certain amount over 1.0.

Return on Investment (ROI)

(Total Benefits – Total Costs) ÷ Total Costs x 100 = ROI

Example: ($189,000 - $129,500) ÷ $129,500 X 100 = 46%

This calculations gives a similar result as the Cost Benefit Ratio, but in different terms. This shows that the ROI is 46% of every dollar spent for training — or .46 cents. As with the Cost Benefit Ratio, different organizations have different opinions about what the acceptable ROI should be.

Generating Support

An e-learning project requires the support of many groups throughout the organization. Gathering this support and troubleshooting any issues will help your project flow more smoothly.

Identify Stakeholders

Because e-learning projects tend to be more expensive and more involved than a typical training project, you will often need to involve more people than you are used to. Take the time to figure out who they are before you need them, or before they find you!

Use the following worksheet to identify the different groups who may want to have a say in how the project is handled. It is better to involve too many people than to forget someone with important input.

Figure 2.5 Stakeholder Worksheet

Go to the Resources page at **www.e-LearningUncovered.com** for a printable version of this worksheet.

Who are they?	What do they want?	Why do they want it?

Been There, Done That: The Font Police

A medium-sized financial services firm was making good progress on its first e-learning initiative – a two-hour overview of the company and the industry. When the online draft was posted for internal review, the marketing department took a look and discovered that the interface was not using the most current logo, the company's standard for web fonts, or the correct shade of red and blue, according to published company standards.

These would have been easy changes to make during the design phase. But since production had already begun, the changes were more expensive. The moral of the story: get everyone involved early!!

Recognize Priorities, Motives, Obstacles

Now that you've found them, don't be surprised if they don't all jump up and down for joy about your new project. Take the time to think about the priorities and motives each group might be dealing with and the obstacles that might arise. For example:

- Upper management – Might be hesitant because previous I.T. projects did not result in the benefits promised.

- Training management – May agree with the business case on paper, but they don't want to personally be responsible for the risks.

- Trainers – Might resist because they secretly wonder if their jobs will go away or if they will understand the new technology.

- Information Technology department – May pose objections because they are already overworked and this would be one more system to support.

- Line managers – Might consider this just another management fad that will take up their time.

- Employees – May be uncomfortable with the technology and disappointed that they don't get the "time off" to go to the training classes which they enjoy.

When building the business case, you took the time to analyze the benefits, costs, and risks of the project from your perspective. Take the time to really look at the project honestly from everyone else's perspective. This will help you overcome resistance, remove potential obstacles for these groups, and create a cohesive team.

Educate on Features, Benefits, Costs

From this point until the formal project sign-off, your job is communication. Use your strategic plan, benefit analysis, and other information to educate the key stakeholders on what you are trying to do and why. But also be sure to listen to everyone's input as well. Work hard to distinguish what is a fear and what is a legitimate concern. Be prepared to make compromises or adjustments to make sure everyone's needs are met.

Summary

You may be under pressure to jump into a project quickly so you can be up and running right away. Conversely, you may also be under pressure to document and prove the ROI mathematically that is a year or more until you can even think about beginning. In the end, a balanced approach will help you ensure your e-learning has a strong justification, a feasible plan, and a supportive team. As you do so, keep these key points in mind:

- Understand what you are trying to accomplish and why.
- Link project goals to overall business goals.
- Identify and quantify benefits.
- Identify high-level costs.
- Calculate the return.
- Identify key stakeholders and their motivations.
- Build support.

3

Managing an

e-Learning Project

Any training development project requires strong management skills. But because an e-learning project generally takes more time, more money, and involves more people, an emphasis on proper management is even more important.

From defining and managing the project to budgeting and working with vendors, you'll want to stay on top of all the details to make sure your project is delivered on time, on track, and on budget.

Project Management

Project Management and the ADDIE Model

The ADDIE model (Analyze, Design, Develop, Implement, Evaluate) is widely used to manage training development. While the use of this model helps ensure that you have high-quality, effective training, it doesn't necessarily mean the project itself will be smooth and efficient.

Therefore, a combination of the ADDIE model and the Project Management model can help you create great training while staying on track.

Figure 3.1 The ADDIE Model vs. the Project Management Model

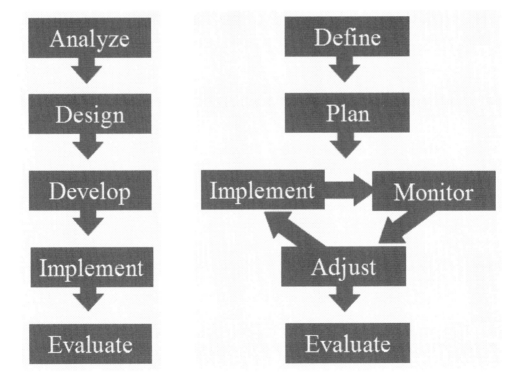

Define the Project

The Definition phase of a project is very similar to the Analysis phase of the ADDIE model – you are trying to find out what needs to be accomplished. From a project management standpoint, you'll want to make sure you know four main things:

- What you are trying to do
- Why you are trying to do it
- Who your customers or stakeholders are
- What success will look like

Steps for Defining Your Project

You'll find tips to help you define the training needs in Chapter 5, The Analysis Phase. However, traditional training analysis does not always consider the business environment – that's where project management comes in.

Create Goals and Objectives

Your specific training goals will be covered in chapter 6. For now, you want to make sure you understand (and everyone agrees upon) the reason why this project is necessary. Think of it as the problem needing to be solved. For example:

- To prepare employees in all 35 locations for the rollout of the new customer relationship software in April
- To provide the same training opportunities for supervisors in our remote locations as the supervisors in our home office

Understand Drivers

It may seem obvious, but make sure everyone is clear about what everyone's motivation is. For example, if your company is starting e-learning because the new CEO thinks it's cool, then you might approach your project one way.

If you are starting e-learning because you want better records because of a painful loss on a related court case, you might manage the project differently. The drivers around the project dictate how much support you get (and keep), what kind of decisions to make, and what kind of trade-offs might be necessary.

Identify Constraints

While it is generally too early to create a detailed schedule and budget, you may be able to identify high-level resource and time constraints. For example, some e-learning projects might have an end-of-the-year goal which is fairly arbitrary – the goal is there to have something to shoot for. But another project might have an end-of-the-year goal because of a new product launch.

Other constraints might be the fact that there is a hiring freeze or that there is or is not money currently in the budget for this project. Understanding these constraints will help you manage the entire project better.

Deliverables for the Definition Phase

Through interviews, negotiations, and brainstorming sessions, you will create a vision for the project. This vision should be documented, shared, and signed off. This documentation may come in the form of a:

- Project Charter.
- Scope of Work.
- Project Definition Statement.

These documents can take any shape or format. If your organization already works with some of these documents on other projects, you might want to borrow their formats. The definition information may also be included in your documentation for the Analysis Phase of the development.

You may also choose to combine some of your project definition information with data you gather during the Analysis Phase. See Chapter 5 for a sample outline.

Figure 3.2 Project Definition Questions

PROBLEM

- What are we trying to do?

- What are we really trying to do?

- What problem<u>s</u> are we trying to solve?

- What caused the problems?

- What client need<u>s</u> will be satisfied?

- What are the benefits?

CUSTOMERS & STAKEHOLDERS STATEMENT

- Who is this for?

- Who else is this for?

- Who else needs to be happy for this to be considered a success?

- Who else might want some input?

- Who else might be impacted?

OBJECTIVES / SCOPE

- What is the desired outcome? (Multiple answers)

- What is the gap between what you want and what you have?

- How will you know you have achieved the desired result?

- What will be different that you can see, hear, touch, measure?

- Which quality criteria are "must do," "should do," and "nice to do"?

- What "extras" might they be unknowingly expecting?

- Will successful completion give rise to other needs?

- What does <u>not</u> have to be done?

- I'm sure there's something else – what is it?

CONSTRAINTS/OBSTACLES

- What prevents us from achieving the objective or makes it difficult?

- What resource and time constraints exist?

- What is the driver? Does everyone agree?

ADDITIONAL ISSUES

- Depend on department, boss, client, company, and personal needs.

Figure 3.3 Sample Scope of Work for an e-Learning Prototype

Analysis

1. Conduct needs assessment to determine:

   - Technology requirements.

   - Desired course features and functions.

   - Profile of typical member of target audience.

   - Overall project scope.

   - Other issues required to make design decisions.

2. Prepare requirements document outlining all needs.

Design

1. Create instructional strategy and outline course features and functions.

2. Make recommendations for decisions on the technology requirements and development platform.

3. Design the interface.

4. Create design standards and templates that can be used by internal or external developers.

5. Document all design decisions.

Development

1. Assemble existing instructional content and create new content.

2. Gather existing media from internal and public-domain sources.

3. Create/acquire additional graphics needed.

4. Build animations, interactions, and assessments.

5. Program the course.

6. Complete all internal, client, and SME reviews as necessary.

Evaluation and Revision

1. Conduct performance testing, usability testing, and user opinion testing.

2. Analyze and summarize feedback.

3. Discuss feedback with development/client team to determine which changes will be implemented.

4. Update design documentation based on changes made through the entire process.

5. Revise estimates for additional courseware designed to the same standards.

Plan the Project

The Planning phase of the Project Management life cycle corresponds closely to the Design phase of the ADDIE model. So while you are designing what the courses should look like, you will need to plan what the project will look like.

This is once again the chicken-and-egg scenario. It will be difficult to finalize decisions about manpower, schedule, and budget until you know that the design will look like. (For example, if the course will include audio or a randomized bank of questions, you

For more details, try
Fundamentals of Project
Management
by James P. Lewis.

will have a higher development effort than if you didn't include either of those.) At the same time, you can't really wait until the design is done to create your project plan, because the Design phase is part of what needs to be managed!!

Most e-learning managers start out with a high-level plan based on early information, and then revise the plan at the end of the Design phase. If you are going to use this approach, make sure the stakeholders know that the first plan is tentative.

A project plan will generally contain the following:

- Task list and schedule

- Resources (money, manpower, equipment)

- Risks (along with mitigation strategies and contingencies)

Sample of Possible Risks for an e-Learning Project

Unavailability of SMEs

Unavailability of IT resources

Managers not giving their employees the time to take the courses

Possible incompatibility of systems

Low bandwidth

Resistance from training team on switch to e-learning

Changing Content

The plan can be developed using a project management tool such as Microsoft Project, or with regular desktop applications such as Microsoft Word or Excel. Additional information on budgets, manpower, and schedules can be found later in this chapter.

Implement, Monitor, and Adjust the Project

In the ADDIE model, implementation means actually launching the training. In the Project Management model, implementation means "doing" the work. This can mean the design, development, and implementation of a training project.

To manage the project effectively, you will want to make sure you have a solid system for tracking progress and dealing with issues. Because e-learning projects are generally more complex than a classroom training project, you may want to use more formal methods of tracking.

Status meetings, status reports, and project management software can all help you stay on top of things. Perhaps just a simple spreadsheet posted on a shared drive can help you keep everything under control.

Be sure to build this project management time into your schedule and development estimates.

Figure 3.4 Development Tracking Sheet

Go to the Resources page at **www.e-LearningUncovered.com** for a downloadable version of this tracking sheet.

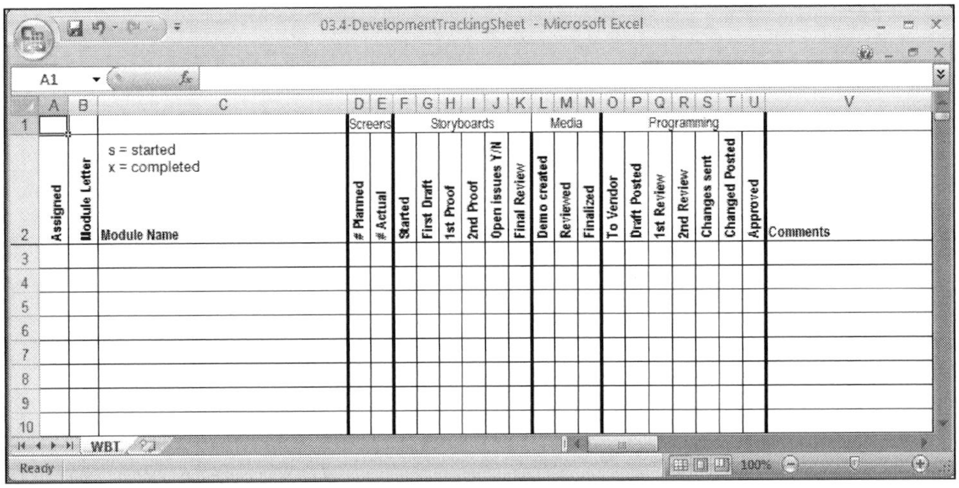

Evaluate the Project

Chapter 11 of this book covers the evaluation of the training. But at the end of a project, take the time to evaluate the process as well. Hold a debrief session and discuss what worked well and what didn't in terms of:

- Team structure.
- Schedule.
- Budget.
- Communication.
- Handling issues.
- Teamwork.
- Customer service.

Conducting these sessions takes discipline. Usually when a project is finished you are already starting your next project! Build the time into your initial schedule to conduct this project evaluation. Every subsequent project will be stronger for it.

Budgeting

Which came first, the chicken or the egg? A similar question can be asked when developing an e-learning budget, "Which comes first, the budget or the specifications?"

It is challenging to put together a detailed budget without knowing what the courses will look like and how it will be developed. Yet it can be a waste of time to get all the answers you need for the specifications without knowing for sure that you even have the money to do the project! This section outlines some general guidelines for you to consider when putting together your budget.

Acquisition Approaches

There are several ways to approach the acquisition of content – and often the choice comes down to the best option financially. So you may need to put together sample budgets for each of the options (either here or during the strategic planning stages) to decide the best way to go.

The following sections address budget issues for each of these options. Refer to Figure 3.5 for non-budgetary issues that relate to this choice.

Figure 3.5 Reasons for the Different Acquisition Approaches

Off-the-Shelf Courseware

❏ You want to get up and running quickly.

❏ You would rather spread your costs out over time.

❏ You do not have a high volume of users.

❏ You are looking for a package deal including LMS functionality.

❏ You are looking for topics that are not industry or company specific.

Custom Development – Contracting Out

❏ You have no e-learning experience on your team.

❏ You expect the workload to be short-lived or inconsistent.

❏ You don't want to take people's focus away from other efforts.

❏ It is easier to find consulting dollars than employee dollars.

❏ You don't want to spend the time or money needed to develop a team.

Custom Development – Developing Internally

❏ You want full control over your content.

❏ You expect a long-term, consistent production effort.

❏ You are able to bring on additional staff.

❏ You are able to provide adequate training for your staff.

Webcasting

❏ Geographic separation is your primary reason for using e-learning.

❏ You do not have a lot of money for development.

❏ You have to get a course ready very quickly.

Types of Expenses

Development Tools

Development tools come in many shapes, sizes...and prices! You can find out more about the tools themselves in Chapter 4, but for now, you will need to include the cost of some or all of these tools into your budget if you will be developing courseware internally.

Course Authoring Tools

Authoring tools are used to actually assemble the courseware. While there are many available options, most of them fall into three main price levels:

Inexpensive: $0 to $650

This category includes standard web development tools such as **FrontPage**, tools to put an existing PowerPoint presentation online, or even shareware programs that cost just a few dollars. Go to the E-Learning Development Resources page at **www.e-LearningUncovered.com** for a list of free tools.

Mid-Range: $650 to $3,000

In this category you'll find pre-packaged software designed specifically for creating e-learning courses. These applications, such as **Lectora** or **ReadyGo**, include e-learning-specific features such as navigation and quizzing – so you don't have to build them from scratch.

This is also the range where you'll find advanced web development tools that can be used for e-learning. A program like **Flash** is more difficult to learn, but allows you to program the courses to do virtually anything.

Expensive: $3,000 and up

It is possible to spend up to $30,000 on an e-learning development tool. Be sure you know what you want and that only these tools will get you there before plunking down that much money. If you are looking for an enterprise-wide license for a number of developers, one of these packages might be the best way to go.

Course Element Tools

In addition to the software you use to assemble the course, you may want specialized software for specific elements. These packages can range from $100 to over $1000. You may want several – or you may not need any. It all depends upon how you design your course and what features are already available in your authoring tool. Some examples include:

- Graphics software, such as **Photoshop Elements** or **Fireworks**.
- Software simulation tools, such as **Captivate** or **Camtasia**.
- Assessment tools, such as QuestionMark **Perception**.
- Game development software, such as **Raptivity**.

You may also want to budget for a graphics library of some sort. You might purchase a selection of photo CDs or perhaps a subscription to a clipart library. Try www.clipart.com or www.fotosearch.com.

Pricing Models: Packaged vs. Hosted

Some development tools are available as a packaged or "shrink-wrapped" solution which means you buy the software, load it, and can use it as long as you like (similar to your word processing or spreadsheet software). Prices in this section reflect that model.

Some tools, however, are available as a hosted or ASP solution. **Atlantic Link** is an example. With this type of solution you don't own the software, but instead you get to use it for a specified period of time (usually one to three years). You can access these from the Web. When you cancel the agreement, you can no longer use the software. If you are considering a hosted solution, make sure you understand all the fees involved. Some companies have a fee to use the software and then additional fees each time the course is accessed.

There are pros and cons to each solution. In general, the initial cost of ownership is lower with a hosted solution, but total cost of ownership is lower with a packaged solution if you plan to use it for more than three years. Also, you need to consider the cost of upgrades for packaged software. Upgrades often cost as much as 20-25% of the original price.

Off-the-Shelf Courseware

You may find that the most cost-effective solution is to purchase a license for pre-existing courseware. As you learned in Chapter 2, these packages generally give you a certain number of "seats" for a certain number of courses for a year. Many of the agreements include LMS functionality, a course authoring tool, or the ability to host and track your own internally-developed courses.

Pricing is generally volume-driven, so your price per user will vary based on the number of people you want to train. In some cases you pay for "seats" whether they are used or not. In other cases, you may only pay for a seat when the course is actually launched.

> *Typical pricing might be $3 to $8 per person per course each year.*

Typical pricing might be $3 to $8 per person per course. So if you have 500 employees and you expect them each to take 10 courses over the year, you might pay $25,000 per year (500 users x 10 course each @ $5 per seat).

There may also be additional fees for:

- Set up and integration with your other systems.
- Training and consulting.
- Use of any LMS or enhanced capabilities.
- The ability to post and track your own courses.
- Maintenance and upgrades.

Synchronous Platforms

If after reading Chapter 2 you've decided that you'd like to use a Webcasting tool, you'll need to negotiate a license price. Check first to see if your company already owns a license for other purposes (perhaps in the Sales Department).

Some solutions, such as **GoToMeeting** and **WebEx**, have per-seat license models that cost around $500-$600 per year for unlimited sessions with 10 participants each. Other subscription solutions, such as Adobe **Connect**, offer hosted packages that range around $350 per month for unlimited meetings with 5 seats or $750+ per month for 10 seats.

If you prefer an "as needed" solution, prices are around 30 to 35 cents per person per minute. This means a 90 minute session with 10 people would cost $297. Many companies will offer volume discounts or let you buy the software so you can host it yourself and have unlimited usage.

Different platforms offer different tools for the Webcast (such as desktop sharing), so you will want to make sure the tool has the functionality you need.

Learning Management Systems & System Integration

An e-learning course generally does not exist in a vacuum. Most companies will want, at a minimum, to log in users and track completion and scores. To do this, you will either need to consider an LMS or build some sort of interface to existing systems. (You can read more about LMSs in Chapter 4.)

System Integration

If you already have systems, such as a Human Resources system, that contain employee data and can accept completion records, you will probably need to budget for an interface between your courses and that system. Based on your situation, the work could be done internally, may need to be contracted out, or may need to be done by the makers of your existing software. Depending on the complexity, this could cost a few hundred dollars or hundreds of thousands of dollars for large, complex organizations.

Learning Management Systems (LMS)

An LMS can simply track completion of individual courses, or it can manage the learning and development of the entire organization. This wide range in functionality comes with an even wider range in costs. Fees could be one-time fee (with maintenance charges per year) if you license the software itself, or yearly if you go with a hosted solution.

Figure 3.6 shows price ranges for LMS implementations. Prices shown are for the cost of a 3-year license, including maintenance and hosting fees (if applicable).

Figure 3.6 Sample LMS Price Ranges

INSTALLED Pricing Ranges

Number of Learners	Price Range
500 learners	$ 9,000 to $ 235,000
10,000 learners	$12,000 to $1,000,000
25,000 learners	$12,000 to $2,000,000
100,000 learners	$12,000 to $5,350,000

HOSTED Pricing Ranges

Number of Learners	Price Range
500 learners	$12,000 – $ 325,000
10,000 learners	$16,000 – $1,100,000
25,000 learners	$16,000 – $2,100,000
100,000 learners	$16,000 – $6,400,000

Inexpensive: $0 to $10,000 total

If you are just interested in offering a catalog, a sign-in page, and course completion records, any web programmer can put something simple together for you. There are some low-cost LMSs available with simple functionality, and some open source options, such as **Moodle**, are available.

Mid-range: $10,000 to $100,000 total

Most LMS implementations fall into this range – but it's a big range! Where expensive solutions were the only real choice a few years ago, more and more mid-range solutions are becoming available. The key to finding a cost-effective solution is to make sure you know what you need (see Chapters 5 and 6) and then look for the tools that give you just that – without a lot of bells and whistles that aren't necessary.

<u>High-end</u>: $100,000 and up

Large corporations interested in full LMS functionality (competencies tied to job title, 360 feedback, performance gap analysis, etc.) might be best served with a high-end solution. Large-scale implementations might run into 6 and even 7 digits.

<u>Hybrid solutions</u>

Remember that some off-the shelf courseware providers and some authoring tools offer LMS capability. Similarly, some LMS packages come with a simple authoring tool and a synchronous platform. Consider whether a package deal might be a good choice for you.

<u>Additional fees</u>

Make sure you know what kind of customization, consulting, integration, and maintenance costs you might be dealing with. In some cases, these could add up to be more than the software itself. Your IT team is likely to be very involved in the implementation, so consider any costs you might incur for their time, as well.

Learning Content Management Systems (LCMS)

Large companies expecting to develop a lot of content, employ many developers, and reuse much of the content between courses may want to purchase an LCMS to manage the content. Costs are similar to an enterprise-wide LMS implementation. As with LMSs, sometimes LCMS capability is packaged with other systems such as an LMS or an authoring tool. (You can read more about LCMSs in Chapter 4.)

Technical Upgrades

You may already have all the technical infrastructure to develop and deliver an e-learning program…but then again you may not. Now is the time to be thinking about what hardware, software, or peripherals might be needed for the company as a whole, or for the individual users.

- <u>Technical platform issues</u> – You may need to budget for additional servers or connectivity.

- <u>User issues</u> – You may need to budget for the users to get speakers, sound cards, video cards, internet connections, earphones, software, or operating system upgrades, or even separate learning workstations.

- <u>IT project time</u> – Based on how your company's accounting works, you may also need to allocate money to pay the IT team to make these upgrades – over and above the cost of the actual equipment. For example, you may need all users to have the Flash player which is free. But the IT department may charge money to push the player down to all workstations.

Internal Team Members or Contractors

Depending on how your company's budgeting process works, you may need to include line items for all the people working on the development. Even if you are outsourcing development, some of your internal team resources will be needed to manage the project and the vendor. You can read more about the manpower needs for your project later in this chapter.

When calculating your budget, you may need to include:

- Salaries.
- Overhead costs and benefits for each team member.
- Possible overtime.
- SME time.

Again, your budget will have to reflect your company's philosophies. In some situations, you may need to include in your budget the wages for the learners while they are taking the courses.

Fees for contractors vary wildly (as do most costs associated with e-learning). Here are some guidelines to get you started.

Instructional Designer: $35 to $85 per hour

Writer/Editor/Proofreader/Researcher: $15 to $35 per hour

Graphic Artist: $15 to $35 per hour

Web Designer: $65 to $150 per hour

Web Developer: $75 to $150 per hour

Outsourcing Development

Asking how much it costs to outsource development is like asking how much is costs to buy a car. The answer is: depends upon what you want.

At the low end, you can pay a few hundred to a few thousand dollars for someone to convert a PowerPoint presentation online, or to put a simple series of text-based web pages online when all the content is already put together. At the high end, you could pay $50,000 and up per finished course hour if you want extensive simulations, high-quality video, or 3-D animations.

> *Most people would pay between $7,500 and $25,000 per course hour.*

Research firm, brandon-hall.com, found prices ranging from $750 to $600,000 per finished course hour!! The average price was $26,618.

Most people, however, should expect to pay between $7,500 and $25,000 per finished course hour. The major variables include:

- The condition of the content – Expect to pay less if all the material is written out somewhere; expect to pay more if all the material is in someone's head.

- The level of interactions and questions – Expect to pay less for straight-forward rollovers and standard question types; expect to pay more for branching scenarios and elaborate simulations.

- The media used – Expect to pay less for stock photography and including video you provide; expect to pay more for custom graphics, animations, professional voice talent, and shooting or editing any video.

- Special programming requirements – Expect to pay less for a template-driven course with pre-set options; expect to pay more for special requirements such as custom learning paths, section 508 compliance, or anything else "really cool" you can think of.

Other Costs

Gather your best brainstormers together to make sure you are considering all your costs. Because each project is different, each budget will be different. Try to conduct your needs assessment (Chapter 5) before committing to your budget. You may uncover additional costs:

- Video footage

- Professional voice talent for audio

- Implementation and promotional costs such as a logo or marketing materials

- Training for your team in e-learning design

- Cost of software or hosting solutions to support blogs, wikis, etc.

- Anything else you can think of!!

Resources

If you are creating an internal development team, you will want to make some important decisions about who should be involved – and to what degree.

Skills Needed

Regardless of how big or small your development effort is, an internal development team needs to possess certain skills. For a large development team, you may need several people for each role. For a smaller team, you may need to find one person who can wear all or most of the hats, perhaps supported by contractors or vendors to fill the gaps. You may need to hire someone specifically to fill a certain role or send a team member to specialized training to learn a new skill.

> *e-Learning development takes various specialized talents. Based on your course design, you may need to budget for the following areas:*
>
> | | |
> |---|---|
> | *Instructional Design* | *Graphic Design* |
> | *Subject Matter Expertise* | *Quality Assurance Testing* |
> | *Research* | *Online Instruction* |
> | *Writing* | *Project Management* |
> | *Proofreading* | *Voice Talent* |
> | *Editing* | *Audio Recording and Editing* |
> | *Programming/Course Assembly* | *Video Production and Editing* |

Figure 3.7 Sample Budgeting Worksheet

Go to the Resources page at **www.e-LearningUncovered.com** for a printable version of this worksheet.

Item	Per Unit Cost	# of Units	Total Cost
LMS			
Initial License			
Maintenance Fees			
Customization/Installation			
IT Costs			
Additional Servers			
Additional Computer Kiosks			
Headsets			
New Training Dept. Work Station			
Development Tools			
Authoring Tools			
Graphics Library			
Audio Recording Equipment			
Training on New Tools			
Contractors			
Proofreaders			
Flash Designers			
Consultant for First Course			
Manpower			
LMS Administrator			
LMS Data Entry Specialist			
IT Implementation Assistance			
Help Desk			
Project Manager			
Subject Matter Experts			
Course Developers			
Students Wages During Course			
Additional Costs			
Program Promotion/Launch			
TOTAL			

Timelines

Development Ratios

When creating initial estimates for first-time projects, you will probably need to rely on industry averages. For straightforward courses with content well defined using simple media, you might expect to spend 40 hours to create every 1 finished hour of courseware. For high-end courses or development that involves full analysis and content gathering, you may spend 200 or more hours for 1 hour of courseware.

The biggest variables surrounding how long it will take to create a course are the same variables that affect the cost of a course:

- The condition of the content

- The level of interactions and questions

- The media used

- Special programming requirements

The best way to estimate the timeline for any project is to break it down into little pieces. The task of estimating a whole project may seem daunting, but you might have a better "feel" when estimating individual sections of the project. Based on what you know about your project, your team, and your environment, perhaps you can make up a chart similar to the one in Figure 3.8.

Turnaround Time

Even if a course takes 40 hours to develop, don't expect it to be finished in a week! Turnaround time will be based largely on:

- <u>The percentage of time each team member can devote to the project</u> – Ask yourself how much time they spend on other projects, on administrative tasks, in departmental meetings, etc.

- <u>The number of people on the project</u> – Each time the project has to pass from one person to another, you are likely to lose a little time.

- <u>Your review cycles</u> – Each time your customers (internal or external) and/or subject matter experts need to review the course, you may need to add another week. At the beginning of a project you may hear that two-day turnaround times are promised, but that may not happen.

- <u>The experience level of the people on the project</u> – For an established team that works well together, a typical one-hour course might take 8 weeks to turn around.

Fig. 3.8 Sample Development Ratio Chart

Task	Ratio to develop 1 course hour
Gather Content	12 to 1
Write storyboards	15 to 1
Review internally	4 to 1
Make changes	3 to 1
Make changes from external review	3 to 1
Find, create, prepare media	15 to 1
Assemble course	8 to 1
QA internally	4 to 1
Make changes	2 to 1
Make changes from external review	3 to 1
Sub-Total	**68 to 1**
Project Management	Add 10%
Total	**76 to 1**

NOTE: These are only sample figures. You will need to estimate your own ratios based on what you know about your project.

As you begin your project, you'll want to keep detailed records about the production process so you can create more accurate estimates for future development.

Your First Courses

Your first few courses will take considerably longer than later courses. Many design and technology decisions need to be made; many processes need to be established; and much organizational coordination needs to take place.

The Analysis and Design phases for your first course might take between 6 weeks and 3 months – even more if you run into obstacles or if you need to first implement an enterprise-wide system such as an LMS in a large company.

Fig. 3.9 Sample Timeline for First Course

Week 1	**Analysis**
	Project kick-off meeting conducted
	Assessment completed
	Requirements document draft delivered
Week 3	Requirements document approved
	Design
	Features list submitted
	Features list approved
	Interface designs submitted
	Interface design approved
	Design document submitted
Week 6	Design document approved
	Standards and templates submitted
	Standards and templates approved
	Development
	Development began
	Prototype delivered
	Prototype approved
Week 8	**Evaluation**
	Evaluation kicked-off
	Testing completed
	Evaluation summary completed
	Re-design recommendations submitted
	Re-design decisions made
	Revised prototype completed
	Revised prototype approved
	Documentation updated
	Cost estimates for Phase 2 delivered
Week 10	**Phase 1 Complete**
	Source code and documentation delivered

LMS/LCMS Implementations

If you will be purchasing an LMS, LCMS, or other enterprise-wide system, you may want to set up a separate project plan just for that. Hosted solutions are generally quicker to set up than packaged solutions. Depending upon the complexity of the tool and the complexity of your systems, an LMS implementation can take as little as a few days or up to six months or longer.

Working with Vendors

An e-learning project may include vendors to provide software, hardware, consulting, or development. Selecting these vendors is an important decision and might best be treated as its own project.

Caveat Emptor

Caveat Emptor: Let the buyer beware. There is a lot of money being spent in the e-learning marketplace. Fortunately, there are a lot of reputable, qualified vendors out there who do a great job. But then there are some who just aren't very good at what they do. And, unfortunately, there are a handful who are just in the marketplace to cash in.

Part of what makes the selection of an e-learning vendor challenging is the fact that you may not know enough to know when a vendor is good, when they are operating outside of their expertise, and when they are about to rip you off.

Your best protection against picking a bad vendor is doing your homework: making sure you know what you do and don't want, and taking a systematic approach to vendor selection. Your best protection against having a project go sour because of a vendor is to make sure you manage the relationship formally.

RFIs and RFPs

Requests for Information (RFI) and Requests for Proposal (RFP) are the two primary tools you can use to select a vendor of any kind.

In general, an RFI is used for preliminary research to help you identify which vendors offer the type of product or service you want and what the general costs and turnaround times would be. RFIs are useful when you are in initial planning stages. Perhaps you don't know exactly what you want, but you want to get at least a general idea of what is out there so that you can sketch out a preliminary budget. This can help you decide if you even want to move forward with the full planning process.

RFPs are more formal documents that specifically list what you want and help the vendor provide a specific, binding proposal.

Creating an RFI

RFIs are fairly simple to put together because they are based on general project goals, rather than detailed specifications. Create a document that outlines:

1. Information about your company and audience.

2. What you are trying to accomplish.

3. The type of product or service you are looking for.

4. Any specifications you do already know.

5. How you want them to respond.

For example, you might create a simple document that explains:

1. You are a small manufacturing firm with 1,250 employees in 8 offices throughout the Northeast.

> **Been There, Done That: Tips for Creating an RFI**
>
> *You may end up wading through pages and pages of marketing language trying to search for answers to your questions. To make your job simpler, be very specific about how you want them to respond:*
>
> - *Provide a form with simple yes and no questions. (Example: Is your system Section 508 complaint?)*
>
> - *Set a page limit.*
>
> - *Provide an outline for them to use when writing their response.*
>
> - *Let them know that an average price or price range is <u>required</u>.*

2. You are looking at offering online safety training for all employees. (You can list the specific topics you are interested in.)

3. You want a vendor with existing courseware that you can license.

4. You would like their system to pull from your ADP employee database and provide reports on completion and test scores. The courses can not require audio because the computer workstations do not have soundcards or speakers.

5. You would like them to respond via e-mail within 2 weeks and provide their list of titles, operating requirements, tracking capabilities, and a link to a sample course, and an average, non-binding price for the type of arrangement you are looking for.

The entire document may only be a few pages long. Remember, you are just trying to gather information to help you plan.

Creating an RFP

Benefits

While putting an RFP together can take a lot of time and effort, it will pay off. Using a formal proposal process helps you:

- <u>Increase competition</u> – You can send your requests to any number of companies to increase your chances of getting a great vendor and a good deal.

- <u>Ensure apples-to-apples comparisons</u> – To really evaluate the differences between vendors, it helps to compare the same thing! Using a formal proposal process ensures that you are comparing like products and services.

- <u>Clarify your own needs</u> – The act of writing the RFP is valuable in and of itself. Even if you never send the RFP out, you will have learned a lot about your project and what you are trying to accomplish.

- <u>Formalize the agreement</u> – The RFP and the resulting proposal spell out the details of the relationship. Often the final contract will refer to the RFP or the proposal, rather than repeat all the details. Having everything spelled out in writing helps eliminate surprises.

Planning the RFP

An RFP asks for a specific, binding proposal. In order for a vendor to respond accurately, you will need to provide a lot of detail. It can be very time consuming to create an RFP, which may range anywhere from 5 to 500 pages! (Most projects would need about 10 to 30 pages.) The good news is that if you've done your homework in planning out your project, your Statement of Work and Requirements Document can easily be converted to an RFP.

But what if you don't know all the details about what you want, and that's part of what you want the vendor to help you with? You have two options.

One is to treat the analysis and design phases as a separate project with a separate contract, price, and schedule. This works well with custom development projects. You could end up with a requirements definition, design document, and about 30 to 60 minutes of content. From there, you create a separate RFP and contract for the full development based on what you have learned.

Another is to work with the vendors to help you determine what you need and help you write the RFP. But be careful! Many salespeople are trained to convince you they have exactly what you need! If you go this route, make sure you talk to several vendors so you get different perspectives.

Sample RFP Outline for Custom Course Development

Background
    Company Profile
    Audience Profile
    Project Goals
Statement of Work
    Course Length
    Course Features and Functions
        Interface
        Menus and Navigation
        Interactions
        Additional Features
    Media Elements
    LMS Integration
    Responsibilities
        Client
        Vendor
    Technical Requirements
    Review Cycles
    Deliverables
        Major Milestones
        Project Schedule
Terms
    Payment Terms
    Ownership
    Confidentiality
Instructions to Proposer
    Proposal Contents
        Cost
        Experience
        Technical
        Samples
        References
    Submission Guidelines
Selection Criteria
Contact Information
Appendix A
    Course Module Breakdown
Appendix B
    Example of Existing Content

What Should Be Included

Major RFP elements will be the same regardless of the type of project.

- Company Background
- Project Overview
- Terms
- Scope of Work or Product Requirements (pulled from your internal documents)
- Instructions for Submission

Specific elements will vary based on the type of project (LMS selection, custom course development, etc.).

Double-checking Your RFP

The most common problems with RFPs include lack of input from all parties (such as IT), sketchy details about the project and what is expected, and unclear guidelines about how the vendor should respond.

To help reduce these problems, get all major stakeholders to sign off on the request and have someone who isn't close to the project review the document to make sure it is clear.

Evaluating Vendor Responses

The review process may consist of reading proposals, reviewing demos, listening to presentations, calling references, even evaluating prototypes created just for you.

The best time to think about how you want to evaluate the vendors is when you are creating the RFP. You want to make sure you ask them for everything you want to know. Don't just assume they will provide samples and references – ask!

Decide who should be involved in the selection process. Do you want an end-user to review the demo? Do you want an IT representative to confirm the technical details and ask any follow-on questions? Do you want the legal department to review the terms and even the courseware?

Determine your selection criteria and rank them. You may have "must-have", "should-have", and "nice-to-have" criteria. Then create a spreadsheet or chart to evaluate each vendor according to the criteria.

Tips for Working with Vendors

Get everything in writing.

If the sales person makes promises over the phone – make sure it gets in the contract. During development, always keep your design document and other guidelines up-to-date with anything the vendor promised they would do.

Put protections in the contract for you!

If the vendor supplies the contract, make sure you are protected. Are there cancellation and privacy clauses for you, or just them? Are there late fees if you don't pay on time, but no penalties if they don't deliver on time?

Figure 3.10 Sample Evaluation Spreadsheet for Off-the-Shelf Content

Criteria	Points	Vendor A	Vendor B
Course Offerings	*150*	*100*	*150*
Course Quality	*200*	*175*	*130*
LMS Capabilities	*100*	*75*	*75*
Company Stability	*125*	*75*	*100*
Project Management Ability	*50*	*50*	*40*
Customer Service	*100*	*100*	*80*
Technical Support	*75*	*75*	*40*
Price	*200*	*175*	*100*
TOTAL	***1000***	***825***	***715***

> **Been There Done That: A Bankruptcy Horror Story**
>
> *A customer had a great relationship with its vendor. Together they created a series of video-streaming courses on management topics. The vendor hosted the courses for a fee. A year later, the vendor went bankrupt and its assets were sold at auction. Unfortunately, the vendor kept copyright and source code for the courses, so they, too, were sold at auction. The new vendor got all the content, but was not bound to the original terms of the contract. The customer then had to negotiate with the new company for the right to access their own courses.*

Know what happens if the vendor goes bankrupt.

The dot-com world is not 100% stable. If your vendor goes out of business, find out what will happen to your courses, your content, your private company information. Put provisions in the contract that protect you.

Keep a single point of contact.

Negotiate for a single project manager and try to interview that person before the contract is signed. The sales person may be great, but that isn't the person who will be helping you day in and day out.

Keep ownership of copyright, data, and source code.

For an LMS project, make sure you will always have access to your completion records. For custom-developed courses, make sure you retain copyright and negotiate to keep the source code. (You may have to pay extra for the privilege.)

Manage changes on your end.

The farther into a project you make changes, the more expensive it will be for you. Take the time to conduct thorough reviews on your end so needed changes don't come back to bite you later. (For example, make sure the marketing department sees the interface when you are in prototype phase instead of when you are ready to launch. Make sure the subject matter experts see the content in storyboard phase instead of when the online draft is posted.)

Have regular progress updates.

Whether you use written reports or weekly conference calls, take the initiative to stay on top of the milestones.

Make payments milestone-based instead of time-based.

If the contract has calendar-based milestones, you could end up paying for deliverables that haven't been delivered! And always hold the last chunk of money (10% to 25%) until EVERYTHING is delivered. (Be good to your vendor, though. If there are long schedule delays that are your fault, find a way to pay the vendor for work they have completed.

Be wary of proprietary code.

If a vendor uses proprietary software, you may forever be tied to that vendor and may not be able to change your courses or move them to a different platform.

Be a good customer.

Customers tell horror stories about vendors. But vendors tell horror stories about customers! Be respectful of their time and efforts by honoring your end of all the agreements. Be realistic when expecting them to make changes and corrections because you've changed your mind or you missed something.

Summary

Great e-learning projects don't just <u>happen</u>. They are expertly defined, planned, implemented, and evaluated. By adding project management tools to your toolbox, you will increase the efficiency of the process and the quality of the end product.

Tools of the Trade

Newcomers to the world of e-learning can easily be overwhelmed by all the technology decisions they have to make, the number of choices available, and the terminology they may not be familiar with. This chapter will help you understand what tools you may need to acquire to create or manage an e-learning program.

You will learn about tools that help you:

- Build your courses as a whole (authoring tools).
- Build individual elements to be included in your course (element tools).
- Create and deliver a Webcast (Webcasting tools).
- Build a virtual classroom environment (virtual classroom tools).
- Track and manage your learning and training information (LMS and other information management tools).

This information works in conjunction with information in other chapters. Chapter 5, covering the analysis phase, will help you understand what sort of hardware and software needs your company has. Chapters 6 and 7, discussing the design phase of the project, will help you determine what specific features you want to incorporate into your courses. Making these decisions will help you know what the best tools are to meet your needs.

Authoring Tools

What is an authoring tool? Definitions may vary some based on who you ask. For the purposes of this book, an authoring tool is the software you use to assemble the course as a whole. It is the tool you would use to place all your course elements (text, graphics, questions, etc.) and turn individual screens into a complete course (pages, navigation, menus, buttons, etc.).

> *An authoring tool is the software you use to assemble the course as a whole.*

Authoring tools have a variety of different features, come in a wide variety of prices, and require different levels of skill. Some tools are very simple to use with templates, wizards, and features that work just like common business software such as Word or PowerPoint. Other tools allow for greater design flexibility but are more difficult to learn – some even requiring programming knowledge.

Selecting the right tool involves consideration of the price, time for development, the level of skill of your users, and the features you want to include in your course.

Classifications of Authoring Tools

Web Authoring

An e-learning course can be considered a type of Website or Web page. Because of this, any tool that can be used to create a Website can be used to create an e-learning course – even if the course will be delivered on CD instead of over the Internet.

Web authoring tools can be a good choice because they are widely used. This means it is easy to find training on how to use the software and easy to find team members who already have the needed skills. You may even have people in your company already (such as in the I.T. or marketing departments) who know how to use the software.

The disadvantage of Web authoring tools is that they are not designed specifically for e-learning. Therefore, many of the course elements have to be custom built, or you would need to buy third-party software to get around this issue and build some of the course structure for you.

HTML Editors

An HTML editor is a software package that allows you to build HTML pages either by creating the code yourself, or by designing the pages visually and allowing the software to create the code behind the scenes for you. The most common HTML editor on the market is Adobe **Dreamweaver**, which has an available extension you can download called **CourseBuilder** that makes it easier to create e-learning.

Courses created with an HTML editor tend to be low-bandwidth, easy to update, and very compatible on different operating platforms. In addition, Web programmers can use programming languages (such as **JavaScript**) to create advanced features.

Media and Application Tools

For more advanced interactivity and media, you could consider using more advanced Web applications such as Adobe **Flash**. These programs are designed to create slick visual presentations and are even used to build new software programs. The capabilities are almost endless, but the learning curve is extensive. **Flash CS4** comes with learning interactions to make it easier to create e-learning than in previous versions.

Course Authoring

Years ago, you had to have programming skills to create any sort of computer-based training. However, there are now more and more tools that are built for the non-techie. These systems are often template- or form-based and very easy for someone to learn and use.

These tools, such as Trivantis **Lectora Publisher** and Rapid Intake **ProForm**, are easy to learn and use. They can be used in a rapid development environment, when you don't have dedicated programmers on staff, and especially when you want subject matter experts to help build the content.

The downside of such tools is that you are locked into the features that come with the software and may not get every feature you want.

PowerPoint Conversion Tools

Several tools on the market automatically convert documents created in traditional desktop software such as Microsoft **Word** or **PowerPoint** into an online course. Many of the software packages listed in the previous sections have the ability to import content from these programs, but there are also tools that allow you to author 100% in **Word** or **PowerPoint**.

Some of these conversion tools simply convert the **PowerPoint** document to a **Flash** file or other Web-enabled format. While this doesn't make for very interactive learning, converting the file to **Flash** makes it a much smaller file and makes it accessible to more people (since 98% of computer users already have the **Flash** plug-in). Examples include Presentation Pro **PowerCONVERTER**, and FlashDemo **FlashPoint**.

Other conversion tools let you add e-learning elements such as interactions, quizzing, and tracking, available on a new menu/ribbon in your **PowerPoint** software. Two examples are Articulate **Presenter** and Adobe **Presenter**.

These tools allow for the shortest learning curve and development time, and allow any number of end users to create content. The downsides are that you are limited to the templates and features available and that the final product may really look more like an online presentation than online learning.

Features of Authoring Tools

Chapters 6 and 7 will help you make decisions about what features you want to build into your courses. One constraint on those decisions will be what your authoring tool can do. Figure 4.1 is a list of many possible features that might be included in an authoring tool. Use it to create your wish list, to help you create an RFP, to compare and rank similar products, or to make design decisions.

Checklist Terminology

- <u>SCORM/AICC</u> – Interoperability standards that ensure e-learning products work together. For example, a SCORM-compliant course should successfully send data to a SCORM-compliant LMS. SCORM and AICC are two different standards that aim to accomplish the same thing.

- <u>Section 508</u> – A federal law for accessibility of electronic communications to people with disabilities. If a course is Section 508 compliant, it meets the guidelines for people with visual, auditory, or motor disabilities.

- <u>Packaged vs. Hosted</u> – Packaged software is software that you purchase, install, and can use as much as you want. Microsoft Word is an example of packaged software. Hosted (or ASP) software is hosted by the vendor and you pay for access to it for a set period of time. There may also be fees to access it.

Figure 4.1 Course Authoring Tool Checklist

Go to the Resources page at **www.e-LearningUncovered.com** for a downloadable version of this checklist.

Feature	Importance	Tool 1	Tool 2
General			
Company name			
Website			
Access to demo			
Packaged or hosted			
Purchase price			
Other fees			
Training provided			
Support provided			
Can be bought alone (not with LMS)			
Company Information			
Years in business			
# of users			
Year this tool was released			
Year this version was released			
Media			
Audio			
Accepts audio files (which formats?)			
Player(s) used to play audio			
User can turn audio on/off			
Lets you record audio			
Lets you edit audio			
Lets you compress audio			
Has audio clip library (music, effects)			
Video			

Chapter 4

Feature	Importance	Tool 1	Tool 2
Accepts video files (which formats?)			
Player(s) used to play video			
Graphics			
File types accepted			
Can crop graphics on-screen			
Can re-size graphics on-screen			
Can add alt-tags to graphics			
Tool to create graphics			
Tool to edit graphics			
Comes with clip-art library			
Other			
Built-in static screen capture tool			
Built-in computer simulation tool			
Built-in animation features			
Other built-in tools			
Accepts Flash files			
Questions			
Question Types			
Multiple choice – single correct answer			
Multiple choice – multiple correct answer			
True/False			
Matching			
Drag-and-drop			
Label a diagram			
Put things in order			
Click somewhere on a graphic			
Fill-in-the-blank (single correct option)			
Fill-in-the-blank (multiple correct options)			
Likert scales (surveys)			
Games, puzzles, etc.			
Short answer			
Essay			
Quiz Placement			
Embedded throughout course			
Course pre-test			
Module pre-test			
Course post-test			
Module post-test			
Randomization			
Pull from randomized bank of questions			
Randomized bank pulls one question per Objective			
Order of questions randomized			
Order of options randomized			

Feature	Importance	Tool 1	Tool 2
Remediation			
Custom remediation per question			
Custom remediation per option			
Wrong answer takes you back to learning page			
Suggests areas to study again			
Can include a hint			
Course branches based on response			
Remediation can be immediate (per screen)			
Remediation can be delayed (per course)			
Remediation can be turned off			
Question options			
Allows graphics on question screens			
Can designate number of attempts allowed			
Questions linked to objectives			
Questions can be given a weight			
Customizable pass percentage			
Partial credit for questions			
Timed quizzes			
Course Structure and Design			
Industry Standards			
AICC compliant			
IMS compliant			
SCORM compliant			
Section 508 compliant			
LMSs integrated with successfully in the past			
Navigation			
Forced navigation possible			
Flexible navigation possible			
Forced navigation for first pass through with flexible navigation after course is finished			
Pre-test with test-out capability			
Pre-test with custom learning path			
Custom learning paths based on log-in			
Require screen to be finished before Advancing			
Number of outline levels per course (course, module, lesson, page, etc.)			
Interface Design			
Customizable screen size			
User-selected full media vs. text-only option			
Course menu always available			
Heading includes course/module title			
Interface templates available			
Supports foreign character sets			

Feature	Importance	Tool 1	Tool 2
Output Options			
Proprietary players required			
Standard players required for no-media version			
Output to Web			
Output to CD			
Output to print			
Output to hand-held			
Output to other formats			
Typical files size per page/per course			
Can play on Mac, PC, Unix, others			
Can play on I.E., Firefox, others			
Course Features			
Bookmarking – automatic/user defined			
Glossary			
FAQ page			
Documents page (pdfs, etc.)			
Screen counter			
Notes page			
Print			
Help			
Send e-mail to designated mentor			
Course evaluation			
Search tool			
Hyperlinks (within course, to Web, to documents)			
Screen Layout			
Use of formatting styles			
Multiple template options			
Roll-over screen templates			
Pop-up screen templates			
Create your own templates			
Development Process & Tools			
Storyboarding tools			
Import content from Word			
Import content from PowerPoint			
Import content from other formats			
Supports learning objects			
On-screen editing and change tracking			
Version control/check-out process			
Other collaborative development features			
Spell check			
File management			
Ability to custom program with standard programming languages (JavaScript, etc.)			

Feature	Importance	Tool 1	Tool 2
Software available in different languages			
Component library to house course elements used frequently			
Error checker/de-bugging feature			
Utility to help upload files to server			
Intangibles			
Easy to learn			
Easy to use			
Flexible			
Finished courses look professional			
Technology Requirements			
Server Requirements			
Developer Requirements			
User Requirements			

Element Tools

While an authoring tool helps you assemble your course as a whole, you may also need additional tools to help you with individual elements of the course. These elements can then be pasted or imported into your authoring tool. In some cases, your authoring tool may have the capability to create these elements and you wouldn't need a separate tool.

Graphics

At a minimum, you will want the ability to crop and re-size graphics and change the file type. Many authoring tools have this capability, but some do not. For the more ambitious, you may want the ability to edit or create graphics yourself.

Photo Editing Software

In addition to cropping and re-sizing graphics, you may want the ability to edit or manipulate graphics. For example, in a course on customer conflict, you may want to find a picture of an angry customer and make the whole photo red. Perhaps you would like to create a photo collage for a title graphic. Or maybe you returned from a photo shoot from your manufacturing floor and you need to lighten up some of the pictures.

Photo editing packages such as Adobe **Photoshop/Photoshop Elements** or **Microsoft Office Picture Manager** give you the ability to modify and enhance photos and other graphics.

Graphics Creation Software

You may want the ability to custom-create graphics. Perhaps you want to create a cartoon character to serve as the "host" of the course. Maybe there are diagrams or processes you need to illustrate, or maybe you want to create your own interface buttons. Your choices include:

- Illustration software such as Adobe **Illustrator**.
- Photo editing software (some have drawing capability).
- End-user business applications. (Diagrams can be created in **PowerPoint** and then saved as an image.)
- Animation software. (Many packages such as Adobe **Flash** can work as a drawing tool.)

Interactions and Animations

Once again, the authoring tool you use may provide the ability to create the interactions (such as a roll-over screen) and animations (such as a moving diagram of a chemical or manufacturing process) you want. However, the use of animation software often allows you to create more advanced, more flexible, and more creative interactive elements. Adobe **Flash** is, by far, the industry standard for creating more custom interactions. Another option is using a template-based interaction software, such as Articulate **Engage** or **Raptivity**, that allow you to easily add your content to the template to significantly decrease development time.

Simulations

Computer Simulations

When creating courses designed to teach software applications (such as an order processing or customer relations management software), you can include on-screen simulations of how the software works. You can even create practice or testing sessions where the student gets to try the steps themselves.

These simulations (whether for demonstration, practice, or testing) can be custom programmed in tools such as **Flash**. However, special tools are available that make it much quicker and easier for an end-user to create these simulations. With tools such as Adobe **Captivate**, Qarbon **ViewletBuilder**, and TechSmith **Camtasia Studio**, you can create a software simulation in less than an hour.

Business and Technical Simulations

One way to make sure your students know how to apply what they have learned back on the job is to create a real-world simulation. These simulations may just be a series of screens outlining a situation, followed by some multiple-choice questions. This type of simulation or scenario can often be done in your authoring tool.

However, some software packages are available that allow you to create more complex and interactive business simulations where the students control variables, make decisions, and see the impact of their choices. Tools include Forio **Broadcast** and PowerSim **Software Studio**. Some companies (such as Forio or ExperiencePoint) have pre-made simulations you can integrate into your courses.

In addition to these choices, there may be software or pre-made simulations specific to your industry. For example, Brooks Automation **AutoMod** software lets you create simulations for the manufacturing industry. It may be worth the time to conduct an online search or to check with your professional associations to see if any such tools exist for your industry.

Another option is to set up a simulation in a virtual world, such as **Second Life**, so people can interact with others online.

Assessments

Most authoring tools, learning management systems, and learning content management systems have the ability to create tests and assessments. You may want to look at software specifically designed for that purpose.

Quizzes and Tests

Tools such as QuestionMark **Perception**, **ExamBuilder,** and XStream Software **RapidExam** all allow you to create and manage tests and exams.

Games

If you'd like to get more creative with your quizzing and assessments, you may want to consider software that lets you create online games. There may be game capabilities in your authoring tool or in regular assessment software, or you can look at tools designed specifically for games such as C3 SoftWorks **Bravo**, Harbinger Group **Raptivity**, **games2train.com**, or LearningWare Inc. **GameShow Pro**.

Audio and Video

In many ways, audio and video are a whole world of their own. If you plan to record and edit your own audio and video, you may need to acquire both equipment and software to do what you want to do. At the simplest level, you may be able to record audio clips in your authoring tool or even in **PowerPoint**. This is a quick and easy way to record, but there are limited editing options. You might need to re-record whenever there is a change or a mistake.

There are some tools such as Microsoft **Windows Movie Maker**, Adobe **Premiere/Premier Elements** and **Adobe Director** that provide a nice balance of capability and ease of use.

On the high end, you could purchase very expensive equipment to record, mix, and edit audio and video. Unless you have a large-scale production effort or other needs in the company for similar services, it is often best to contract out any high-end media production.

Synchronous Platforms

You learned in chapter 1 that synchronous learning occurs when an instructor and students are together at the same time – but not necessarily in the same physical place. One of the most common methods of synchronous e-learning is through Webcasting.

A Webcast is an event where students log into a session and an instructor presents live content. While a Webcast could technically be one-way communication where the instructor presents and the participants just watch or listen, e-learning Webcasts generally include two-way communication, collaboration tools, and interaction. These are the types of tools that will be discussed in this section.

Some of the most popular Webcasting tools on the market are **WebEx**, **Microsoft LiveMeeting**, Citrix **GoToMeeting**, and **Adobe Acrobat Connect**.

Primary Synchronous Features

There are many features common among the major Webcasting platforms. The following section will give you a general understanding of what is included. Refer to Figure 4.2 at the end of the section for a more detailed list of features.

Content Delivery

Content is generally delivered in a Webcast using one or more of the following methods: audio, video, and visuals.

Audio

Most Webcasts include an audio element. This can be done either over the phone or through the internet. If done over the phone, a conference line would be set up, the instructor would teach through the phone, and the participants would listen on the phone. If done through the internet, the instructor would either teach through the phone or through a microphone attached to the computer and the participants would listen through their computer speakers or headphones. The audio could be one- or two-way.

Video

If all participants are using high-bandwidth connections, you could incorporate video into the broadcast. The presenter could hook up a simple Webcam to the computer and the participants could watch a video of the presenter giving the lesson. Some platforms also allow students with Webcams to be seen by the instructor and other participants.

Visuals

The most common form of visual elements used in a Webcast is imported **PowerPoint** slides. The presentation can be created in advance, uploaded into the system, and displayed for everyone attending. Many platforms allow other forms of content to be uploaded, with some even allowing you to create content right in their system.

Application Sharing

Webcasting can be a great choice for teaching a software application. The presenter can pull up any application on his or her desktop and everyone viewing the session can watch whatever the presenter does with the software. Some platforms allow the presenter to turn over control to any of the participants who can then try the procedure themselves.

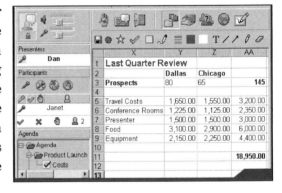

Application sharing can also be used to show any document without having to upload it. For example, you could pull up a report to work on it and everyone could watch and help — allowing for collaboration.

Whiteboards

While the visuals for a Webcast are generally prepared and loaded in advance, whiteboard capabilities let the presenter make marks on any of the slides or on a blank screen. For example, the presenter can draw attention to a certain point by drawing a circle around it or highlighting it in yellow. Some platforms allow any of the participants to use the whiteboard as well.

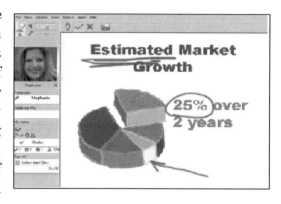

Chat Features

Chat features can be used for communication with the instructor, between students, and for special projects.

Participants can send a message to the instructor to make a comment or ask a question. When the session uses only one-way audio, this is the main way participants can let the instructor know what's on their minds.

If there is two-way audio, students may still choose to send a message to the instructor so they don't have to interrupt or because they want it to be private. Instructors can then either respond through the audio, or send a message back.

Students can also send messages to each other – to the whole group or to individual participants. Finally, the instructor can create "breakout" rooms where certain participants can chat in response to an issue, question, or assignment.

Training Management

Webcasting platforms may come with a full set of tracking and reporting features, similar to what might be found in a Learning Management System. In addition, most systems will help you manage the registration process and help attendees know how to log in when it is time.

Surveys and Polls

In a classroom setting, the trainer will often ask formal or informal questions and get visual feedback from the audience. In a Webcasting environment, there are tools that accomplish much of the same thing.

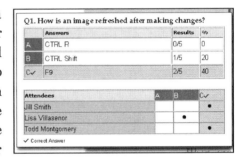

With most platforms, the instructor can ask a question and have participants vote yes or no. Participants click a button to respond and the presenter can tally the results. To help manage questions, the students can click a button to "raise their hand" to let the presenter know they have a question. The hand raising feature can also be used for polling.

Emoticons, or symbols that show expressions, can be used for participants to show how they are feeling. They can click buttons to indicate laughter or applause, for example.

Questions and polls can be created in advance or on-the-fly to get opinions from the audience or to check their knowledge.

Figure 4.2 Synchronous Platform Feature Checklist

Go to the Resources page at **www.e-LearningUncovered.com** for a downloadable version of this checklist.

Feature	Importance	Tool 1	Tool 2
General			
Name of Company			
Website			
Access to Demo			
Hosted, Purchased, or Per Use			
Pricing			
Other Fees			
Training Provided			
Support Provided			

Feature	Importance	Tool 1	Tool 2
Company Information			
Years in business			
# of clients			
Year this tool was released			
Year this version was released			
Registration			
Web-based scheduling and registration			
Online self-registration			
User and event data stored in a database (types?)			
Import users from database or spreadsheet (types?)			
Can limit class size			
Automatic notification to registrants			
Single click access to session from e-mail			
Other special registration features			
Audio/Video			
Voice over IP (audio through the Internet instead of over a phone line)			
Conference bridge			
Simultaneous voices supported			
Video conference capability			
Imbed video files			
Teaching/Content Options			
Whiteboard			
Application demonstration			
Navigate to Websites			
Import content from PowerPoint			
Import content from Word			
Other file types supported			
Templates for creating content in the tool			
Collaboration/Interaction			
Shared whiteboard			
Application sharing			
Group chat rooms			
Breakout or private chat rooms			
Public and private messaging			
Polling			
Surveys			
Quiz questions (question types supported?)			
Threaded discussions/forums			
Web surfing by each participant independently			
Hand raising			
Emoticons (laughter and applause indicators)			
Participants can send anonymous feedback			

Feature	Importance	Tool 1	Tool 2
"Step-out" indicator			
Tracking and Management			
Available reports			
Custom reports			
Report exporting options (.xls, .csv, etc.)			
Interoperability with LMS			
Interoperability with LCMS			
Any desired features from authoring tool list			
Any desired features from LMS list			
Any desired features from LCMS list			
Other			
Recording and archiving of sessions			
(List special archiving features offered)			
Interface available in other languages			
Customizable interface (branding)			
Supports foreign character types			
Supports multiple facilitators			
Note taking capability for students			
E-commerce capabilities			
Content can be pre-loaded on user's machine			
Pre-session features (such as self-paced content or documents)			
Post-session features (such as threaded discussions available after the session)			
Technology Requirements			
Server requirements			
Developer requirements			
User requirement			
User system check prior to launch			
Can operate behind company firewall			

Virtual Classroom Platforms

A virtual classroom is an environment that is both synchronous and asynchronous. It mimics a university-class structure where everyone participates in the course together over a series of weeks. It is synchronous in that there is a beginning and an end with everyone participating together. It is asynchronous in that the actual reading and work can be done at any time within the schedule of the course.

For example, there may be reading and assignments for everyone to complete in week 3 of the course (the synchronous side). But each participant is able to pick whether he or she will complete the work on Tuesday vs. Wednesday morning or evening (the asynchronous side).

One significant difference between the virtual classroom and other instructor-led sessions, such as a Webcast, is that with a virtual classroom environment, the instructor does not usually teach the content personally. The content is usually gathered by the student from a traditional text, online documents, Websites referenced, etc. The instructor is there to facilitate discussion, assign and grade homework and projects, and provide feedback.

Virtual classroom platforms are used almost exclusively in academic environments. **Blackboard** is the most commonly used system.

Note: Many people consider the synchronous tools explained in the previous section to also be called a virtual classroom.

The LMS and Other Management Tools

LMS: Learning Management Systems

Most e-learning initiatives require some sort of learning management. However, that does NOT mean that a formal Learning Management System must be purchased. Full-service Learning Management Systems manage the administration of the training, as well as a number of employee development, learning, and knowledge issues.

Simple Learning Management Systems

At a minimum, you will need a place where the learner can go to find the course and launch it. Most people will want some way to restrict access, perhaps with a log-in and password. And many more still will want to find out who has completed the courses and who has passed the tests.

To gain these functions, you could choose to purchase a Learning Management System, or you could create a Website and database for a simple project. A course catalog could be a simple HTML page and completion data can be sent to a database or even through an e-mail. Most Web programmers could put something simple together to meet the most basic launching and tracking needs.

Advanced Learning Management Systems

Learning Management Systems can also do a lot more. An LMS can:

- Interface between the system you use to keep employee data and your training.
- Automatically manage complex registration issues such as individual catalogs or even course assignments based on the person's role with the company.
- Manage certifications and training that "expires."
- Create assessments and surveys – rather than using your authoring tool.
- Provide advanced reporting on completions.
- Manage other performance and development issues such as skill tracking, performance feedback, and gap analysis.
- Offer social networking and knowledge-sharing features such as personal profiles, blogs, wikis, etc.
- Provide all the same features as an authoring tool, a learning content management system, or a synchronous platform.

Full-service LMS providers include **SumTotal Systems**, **Saba**, and **Learn.com**.

Figure 4.3 Learning Management System Feature Checklist

Go to the Resources page at **www.e-LearningUncovered.com** for a downloadable version of this checklist.

Feature	Importance	Tool 1	Tool 2
General			
Name of Company			
Website			
Access to Demo			
Hosted or Purchased			
Pricing			
Other Fees			
Training Provided			
Support Provided			
Average Time it Takes to Implement			
Company Information			

Feature	Importance	Tool 1	Tool 2
Years in business			
# of clients			
Year this tool was released			
Year this version was released			
Registration and Catalog			
Pulls employee data from HRIS system			
Log in with user name and password			
Secure log-in technology			
Automatic password reminders			
Custom catalog based on log in			
Courses automatically assigned based on log in			
Individual learning plans			
Manager approval required			
Managers assign courses			
E-mail confirmation of registration			
Deadlines assigned for course completion			
Reminders set for upcoming deadlines			
Pre-requisite management			
Searchable index for content			
Courses grouped into content areas			
Can post and track documents other than courseware (PowerPoint, pdf document, etc.)			
Skills and Performance Management			
Certification programs			
Competencies tied to job titles			
Skills assessment/competency gap analysis			
Skills inventory			
360º feedback			
Completion Tracking			
Tracks course complete: Y/N			
Tracks course complete: % complete			
Tracks time spent on each course			
Can print certificates of completion			
Assessment Tracking			
Tracks pass vs. fail			
Tracks pass/fail and grade			
Ability to set pass rate			
Tracks number of attempts			
Keeps all scores (each attempt)			
Keeps only highest score			
Keeps only best score			
Tracks per-question responses			
Psychometric reports			
Reporting			

Feature	Importance	Tool 1	Tool 2
Available reports			
Custom report capabilities			
Web-based reporting			
Ability to export report data (file type options)			
Student transcripts			
Managers can see their employees' data			
Post-training evaluations			
Classroom Management			
Tracks classroom training completion			
Handles classroom training registration			
Manages facility usage			
Manages training equipment usage			
Schedules trainers			
Interoperability/Accessibility			
Interface available in multiple languages			
SCORM compliant			
AICC compliant			
Section 508 compliant			
Authoring tools that have integrated successfully			
LCMSs that have integrated successfully			
Off-the-shelf content that has integrated successfully			
Other			
e-commerce capability			
Chargebacks to individual departments			
Customizable interface (branding)			
Built-in authoring tool (use Fig. 4.1)			
Synchronous/collaboration tools (use Fig. 4.2)			
LCMS capabilities (use Fig. 4.4)			
Social netorking/knowledge sharing			
Technology Requirements			
Server requirements			
Developer requirements			
User requirements			

Implementation Options

The challenge when making decisions about an LMS is to make sure you know exactly what you do and don't need it to do, and then find the right tool. Some companies have spent too much money on systems with features they just don't need. Conversely, other companies have tried a home-grown system that wasn't flexible and scalable enough to meet everyone's needs a year later.

LMS systems vary widely in terms of capabilities, price, and implementation time. A large-scale implementation for a multi-location company with a full-service LMS that needs to integrate into several different systems could take 6 months or more to implement and comes with a 6-digit price tag. Mid-market systems with simpler integration needs might take a few weeks to a few months to implement and comes with a 5-digit price tag. Brandon Hall (www.brandon-hall.com) offers a list of low-cost LMS options.

LCMS: Learning Content Management Systems

A Learning Content Management System may be the most misunderstood of the e-learning tools discussed here. It <u>may or may not</u> have all the features of an authoring tool, an LMS, and a synchronous environment. This section will focus on what makes an LCMS different from the other tools, even though those features might be incorporated as well.

A Learning Content Management System is actually named well – it helps you manage the *content*. While an authoring tool helps you *create* content and a Learning Management System helps you manage the *learning activity*, an LCMS helps you manage the actual *content* itself.

Functions unique to an LCMS include:

- Organized storing, searching, and retrieval of course elements.
- Structuring of content into reusable learning objects that include all training material associated with a given objective – pre-test questions, teaching content, media elements, and post-test questions. (You will learn more about learning objects in chapter 6.)
- Collaborative development tools that help coordinate the production efforts of the development team.

LCMSs are best used for large development efforts that include hours and hours of content, many developers, and the need to re-use content or content elements across courses. Smaller projects may find that an LCMS is not cost-effective and that these functions can be managed through effective file and project management. **Outstart** and GeoLearning **GeoLCMS** are two examples.

Figure 4.4 Learning Content Management System Feature Checklist

Go to the Resources page at **www.e-LearningUncovered.com** for a downloadable version of this checklist.

Feature	Importance	Tool 1	Tool 2
General			
Name of Company			
Website			
Access to Demo			
Hosted or Purchased			
Pricing			
Other Fees			
Training Provided			
Support Provided			
Average Time it Takes to Implement			
Company Information			
Years in business			
# of clients			
Year this tool was released			
Year this version was released			
Content Authoring			
Built-in authoring tool (use Fig. 4.1)			
Authoring tools that have integrated successfully			
Built-in models for creating learning objects			
Synchronous/collaboration tools (use Fig. 4.2)			
Content Storage			
Types of files accepted (ppt, pdf, etc.)			
Drag and drop content into system			
Type(s) of database(s) used			
Metadata tagging			
Ability to upload existing courseware into system			
Learning content stored separately from interface and navigation			
Follow SCORM guidelines for creating and organizing content			
Use Word styles to organize objects			
Content Reusability			
Reuse of entire courses			

Feature	Importance	Tool 1	Tool 2
Reuse of entire topics/modules			
Reuse of objectives/learning objects			
Reuse of individual pages			
Reuse of individual elements			
Ease of search and retrieval			
Output formats for non-computer based training (such as a student workbook or instructor guide)			
Output to XML, Word, PowerPoint			
Collaborative Development			
Version control			
Change tracking			
Bug tracking			
Developer's notes per screen/element			
Check-in/check-out capability			
Project management/task assignments, etc.			
Development permissions based on log-in			
Tracking of approvals/sign-off			
Ability to send e-mail notifications to developers			
Interoperability/Accessibility			
Interface available in multiple languages			
SCORM compliant			
AICC compliant			
LMSs that have integrated successfully			
Off-the-shelf content that has integrated successfully			
Learning Management			
LMS capabilities (see Fig. 4.3)			
Technology Requirements			
Server requirements			
Developer requirements			
User requirements			

Other Information Management Systems

You may already have systems in place that will help you with the administration of your e-learning program.

HRIS: Human Resource Information System

An HRIS system, such as **PeopleSoft** or **ADP**, generally tracks HR-related employee data such as personal information, salaries, performance, and payroll. These systems sometimes take different names such as ERP (Enterprise Resource Planning) and HCMD (Human Capital Management and Development).

Some of these systems have the ability to track training data and can therefore serve as your LMS. Older systems may not be built specifically to handle e-learning – just classroom training – but can perhaps be "tricked" into accepting data for an e-learning course. Newer systems may have e-learning tracking capabilities built right in.

Even if you will have a separate Learning Management System, it will need to "talk" to your HRIS system. You might want your HRIS system to send a file to your LMS once a week or so with updated employee data for log in purposes. Conversely, you may want your LMS to send data back to the HRIS system.

TMS: Training Management Systems

The concept of using software to track training is not new. Today, the term TMS can mean one of two things:

- A system that tracks only classroom training – These systems have been around for years and are still in use today by many companies.
- A system that tracks only e-learning completion – If the system tracks registration, catalogs, log-ins, and completion tracking, some would refer to it as a TMS instead of an LMS. Some people only consider it an LMS if it includes other learning and development capabilities other than course management.

Summary

As you can see, there are many options that allow you to create, deliver, and manage your e-learning. Many products fill more than one purpose, and many companies provide more than one type of product. (Off-the-shelf courseware vendors often have LMS capability, for example.)

It is important to establish up front which features you want, prioritize them based on necessity, and then find the best product to meet your needs and your budget.

5

The Analysis Phase

Since the ADDIE model (Analyze, Design, Develop, Implement, Evaluate) is widely used to manage training development, this book is organized to follow this model.

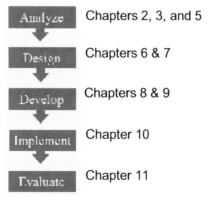

Analyze — Chapters 2, 3, and 5

Design — Chapters 6 & 7

Develop — Chapters 8 & 9

Implement — Chapter 10

Evaluate — Chapter 11

Part of the analysis phase actually took place during your strategy and project planning phases. The analysis continues here as you gather information that helps you make a number of design decisions about your e-learning programs.

The goal of analysis is to ask the right questions and discover information about the business environment, learners, and technology in the organization so you can determine the most effective course design.

On most training development projects, the phases of the ADDIE model are not distinct and finite, but rather they blend together and overlap. As you get more specific in the analysis phase, it is useful to think about how you will use that information during the design phase. For example, you will ask technology questions during this phase so you can make decisions about e-learning format and media usage in the next phase. Analyzing the audience now will help you make decisions about everything from module length to writing style to testing strategies later.

> *The goal of analysis is to ask the right questions.*

Much of the analysis you will conduct would be the same whether you are looking at traditional classroom training or e-learning. If you are not familiar with the process, there are excellent resources to help you understand your needs and goals (such as <u>Rapid Instructional Design</u> by George Piskurich).

This chapter will touch on the elements that are similar to the analysis for classroom training, but will mostly emphasize the elements that are unique to e-learning.

Business Analysis

Any business training, regardless of the format, should fit a specific business need. Conducting a business analysis will not only help you decide whether you need training and what to train on, but will also help you uncover issues that would affect how you structure, present, and test on the material.

The Problem

Training professionals are often given a problem the organization is facing and are told to solve it with training. Since not all problems have training solutions, it is important to thoroughly understand the real problem so you can find the best way to solve it. The questions you need to ask to get to the root of the problem are no different for an e-learning program than they are for a classroom program.

You may have to ask multiple questions (for example, why? how? etc.) and look at all levels of the organization to get details on the pertinent information. Remember that during the analysis phase you are merely asking the questions and documenting the answers. In the design phase you will make the decisions about how to approach the situation.

Figure 5.1 Problem Analysis Checklist

Go to the Resources page at **www.e-LearningUncovered.com** for a downloadable version of this checklist.

Question	Answer
What is the problem?	
What caused the problem?	
Where is the problem (certain department, entire organization, etc.)?	
When did the problem begin?	
Is the problem consistent?	
Has the problem ever occurred before?	
What are the issues that surround the problem?	
Has anyone tried to fix the problem before? If yes, how did they try to fix it and what was the outcome?	
How was the problem discovered?	
What are the consequences if the problem continues?	
What are the benefits if the problem is solved/lessened?	
Are there legal or compliance issues involved?	

Specifically, asking these questions will help you understand:

- Whether training will solve the problem.
- If training won't solve the problem, can it offer an opportunity for improvement?
- Who needs the training.
- Who should be involved in development.
- What the objectives should be.
- What information to include.
- How that information would best be taught.
- If e-learning would be a good format.
- The importance of content review and sound testing.

For example, say you are told that sales have decreased 30% over the last quarter and you need to find the cause. You may find the cause is a change in a customer service policy or perhaps the release of a new product the sales force doesn't really understand how to present to customers.

The first answer would suggest a review of the policy would help most, rather than training. The other answer may mean some quick training is needed on features, along with discussions on how to present the product. If just product knowledge was needed, self-paced training might be effective. If discussion was necessary to help the sales team determine how to apply the information in real-world situations, perhaps a blended solution would work best.

The Business

Understanding the overall business environment will also help you make decisions about how to approach training – classroom or computer-based. Some of these questions may be obvious if you are internal to the organization, but it is still worth the time to document the answers.

You will want to look at the organization as a whole – look at the type of business and how it is laid out so you can later decide how to get the training to the learners. You will see in chapters 6 and 7 that the size and structure of the organization could be a big factor in your choice of a classroom delivery or an e-learning platform.

Figure 5.2 Business Analysis Checklist

Go to the Resources page at **www.e-LearningUncovered.com** for a downloadable version of this checklist.

Question	Answer
What is the business (retail, manufacturing, etc)?	
What types of tasks do the employees do?	
What are the job classes (manager, associate, etc.)?	
How many locations are there?	
How spread out are the locations? Different countries? Time zones?	
What are the different departments?	
How many employees are there?	
What is the business culture?	
What is the turnover rate for the organization?	
Who are the decision-makers in the organization?	
Are there corporate communication guidelines you need to adhere to (fonts, colors, logo usage)?	

Specifically, these questions will help you decide:

- The style and tone of the interface, graphics, and language.

- The best format (classroom, e-learning, or type of e-learning).

- The cost-effectiveness of an e-learning solution.

For example, a traditional, conservative financial institution may not be suited for game-based simulations and an organization with locations throughout the world may not be able to support webcasts because of time-zone differences.

The Learning Environment

Many of the questions that help you make your training decisions may revolve around the learning culture and environment for the entire organization. (More questions will be asked later about the target audience itself.) You will want to gather information about what learning strategies have been used in the past, what has worked, and what hasn't. You may want to find out what made learning successful in the organization and how different strategies were received.

If e-learning has been used by the organization, find out everything you can about what topics were rolled out, how it was designed, and how the learners responded to it.

There may also be requirements that have been put in place about learning – guidelines such as who can take training, for how long, and in what format. Be sure to note whether your answers are true for all training, for a specific course, or for a certain group of courses.

Figure 5.3 Learning Environment Analysis Checklist

Go to the Resources page at **www.e-LearningUncovered.com** for a downloadable version of this checklist.

Question	Answer
How is training perceived in the organization? - By upper management? - By the target audience? - By the supervisors of the target audience?	
What types of training have been used before?	
What types of training have been successful?	
What learning incentives have been used in the past – positive and negative?	
What disincentives to completing training might exist?	
Are there limitations on who can take classes (for example, by job function or job title)?	
Who is in charge of training?	
How much money is in the budget for training?	
Who is most likely to develop the training: training department, contractors, subject-matter experts?	
How often will the material change/need to be updated?	
Do you have mandatory training requirements? Self-imposed requirements?	
Do you have mandatory testing requirements? Self-imposed requirements?	
Do you need to prove to anyone that the training was	

Question	Answer
completed? Passed?	
Are grades important?	
In what ways is training tied to performance (such as bonuses, appraisals, etc.)	
How long can the target audience typically get away for when they need training?	
Should a student pick and choose courses?	
Should a student pick which sections of a course to take?	
Do the students need to take the training even if they know the information?	
Has e-learning been introduced to the organization? With what reaction and result?	
What tracking and reporting needs do you have?	
Do you have certain training that must be taken again annually?	

Knowing the answers to these questions can help you decide:

- Whether e-learning is a good fit.
- How hard you might need to "sell" e-learning to the organization.
- Whether you need an LMS and with what features.
- What kind of navigation and testing to include in the course.
- How long to make each course/module.
- Which authoring tool might be best.
- How you will plan your implementation.

For example, in an environment where front-line supervisors are not very supportive of training, it might be challenging for employees to get away from their work long enough to take an online course. You'll want to consider this when creating your implementation plan.

If you have compliance needs, you may want to set up navigation so that students view every screen of a course whether they know the information or not. In another case, you may allow students to freely pick and choose what they want to learn, or maybe even test out of the information they already know.

Audience Analysis

The audience analysis is where you find information about your learners to understand their ability to take your course and learn the material.

You will want to look at everything from your audience's language ability and computer knowledge to their motivation and existing knowledge on the subjects being taught.

Some additional questions you will want to ask may be decided based on the answers you found when analyzing the business, so remain flexible during the analysis process. For example, you may want to look at the overall demographics for an entire company, but in a global company, you may also want to find information for each individual location. You may find that one branch has something unique that requires special thought in the design phase.

Figure 5.4 Audience Analysis Checklist

Go to the Resources page at **www.e-LearningUncovered.com** for a downloadable version of this checklist.

Question	Answer
Demographics	
What are the different age groups?	
What are their educational backgrounds?	
What is their English proficiency (reading, writing, listening)?	
What other languages are spoken that might be preferable for the training?	
Are there literacy issues?	
What is the reading level of the group?	
Work Environment	
Will students be taking courses from home?	
Will students be taking courses while traveling?	

Question	Answer
Does the environment have interruptions?	
Does the environment have noise?	
Will noise disrupt their environment?	
What shift(s) do they have?	
When will they take the training?	
Computer Knowledge	
Are they comfortable using computers? - What is their computer proficiency? - How is it different within the target audience?	
Are they comfortable with the e-learning format?	
Subject Matter	
What level of knowledge do they already have?	
What experiences have they had with subject?	
Are they likely to need to refer to the material again after training is complete?	
Are they likely to have trouble understanding the information?	
Are they likely to have trouble applying the information?	
Motivation	
How receptive are the learners to training in general?	
How receptive are the learners to THIS topic?	

Question	Answer
Are they being forced to go to training?	
Have you had situations where the students tried to "get around" completing mandatory training?	
Are there concerns about cheating?	
Disabilities/Special needs	
Is there anyone in the target audience with special auditory needs?	
Is there anyone in the target audience with special visual needs?	
Is there anyone in the target audience with special motor skills needs?	

Knowing more about your audience can help you make decisions about:

- What format to use for the training.
- Whether to use fixed versus flexible navigation.
- How to structure testing.
- Whether to make the course Section 508 compliant or perhaps use some of the programming guidelines found in that requirement.
- How to present your information (style, graphics, benefits, language).
- What advanced course features to use or leave out.
- What help features and instructions to use.
- Where the training should take place.
- What information to include, leave out, or allow people to test-out of.

For example, if you have possible issues with motivation and the students have a history of sharing answers on a test to complete mandatory training, you may want to build in a secure password system and a randomized test bank to strengthen the integrity of the test records. If the topic is likely to be met with resistance, perhaps a classroom session or webcast would be best so that the instructor can gauge and respond to that resistance.

Technology Analysis

Analyzing your technology is unique to e-learning over classroom training. For this part of the analysis process, you will want to look at what technology an organization has in place that could support or hinder e-learning.

This analysis can be harder than it looks. It is often easy to find the "norm" for the company, but there may be a few computers, workstations, or just one person who works from home that could make you extend your search for information.

During the technology analysis, you want to find the worst case for each question. For example, the computers may all have sound cards, but 10% don't have speakers. While that doesn't mean you need to design for the 10%, you do need to know this to decide if audio is a viable option.

You will want to work very closely with your IT department, if you have one, so you can make sure you haven't missed anything. They are often your best source of information regarding current technology or restrictions for the course.

Figure 5.5 Technology Analysis Checklist

Go to the Resources page at **www.e-LearningUncovered.com** for a downloadable version of this checklist.

Question	Answer
Technology for Student Computers	
Do they have speakers/headphones?	
Do they have a sound card?	
What is their processor speed?	
What operating system are they using?	
Do they have Internet access?	
What is the browser type and version?	
What is the connection speed?	
What is the screen size?	
How much memory do they have?	
What are their screen colors (number the monitors support)?	
Is video input available?	
Do they have video playback capability?	
What drives are available (CD, floppy, DVD)?	

Question	Answer
Is a printer available?	
Do they have a microphone?	
What version of the Flash player is installed?	
Restrictions	
What is their bandwidth?	
Is there a firewall?	
Can they download/install files?	
Are their guidelines for individual file sizes?	
Miscellaneous	
Will anyone be accessing the courses through a remote network (such as Citrix)?	
Would any information need to move between your course and other systems?	
Would your courses need to be SCORM or AICC compliant?	

Understanding this information will help you make decisions about:

- What authoring tool to use.
- Whether you need to set up dedicated training stations.
- What file size, plug-in, and other design restrictions you might have.
- What type of media can be used.
- What upgrades might be necessary for implementation.

For example, if students are not allowed to download/install files on their computer, some courses will not work. Some off-the-shelf courseware requires files be loaded temporarily to the computer before they are played.

Summary

During the analysis phase you want to gather valuable information that will help you make decisions about your training. You need to ask questions about the problem, business, audience, and technology. Once you have the answer to your questions, you will use the design phase to decide what solutions are best and what your objectives will be. The next 2 chapters explain what to do with the information you have gathered and how to make design decisions that you will use when developing your course.

6

The Design Phase: Broad Strategies

In the analysis phase, you asked a lot of people a lot of questions and documented a lot of answers. Now it is time to turn those answers into a new question: What does this mean for the training? Where the analysis phase was about gathering information, the design phase is about making decisions based on that information.

Many of the decisions are the same regardless of whether you are looking at classroom training or e-learning. However, many of the decisions are unique to e-learning. This chapter will address the broad, overall strategies, and the next chapter will address specific design decisions about course features and functions.

e-Learning and Instructional Design

Within the ADDIE model, the design phase helps you make decisions about whether or not you need training, what you need to teach, and the best way to teach it. You will create a roadmap of what you want to accomplish and how you plan to get there. If the design phase is conducted and documented properly, any training developer could pick up this "roadmap" and begin to develop the training.

There are many interpretations of what steps should be included in the design phase. The most common include:

- Develop learning objectives.
- Determine pre-requisite skills.
- Create a content outline.
- Decide on instructional strategies.
    Presentation of content
    Practice activities
    Assessments
- Choose the right delivery system.
- Create test questions. *(Chapter 7)*
- Decide on course features, functions, and design. *(Chapter 7)*
- Create a design document. *(Chapter 7)*

If you have never developed training before or have never had formal instruction in the training design/development process, you may want to do some research on your own. This book will address many instructional design issues, but is not intended to be an instructional design text. Instead, the goal is to give you a basic understanding of all the tasks you will need to perform, and a deeper understanding of what is unique to the development of an e-learning project.

For example, you could read an entire book just on how to develop instructional objectives – and most of the information would be the same regardless of whether you are creating classroom training or e-learning. This book will show you how the steps to developing objectives relate to e-learning, but not everything you would need to know to create them.

Instructional Design Resources

Big Dog's ISD Page by Don Clark
(http://www.sos.net/~donclark/hrd/sat.html)

Rapid Instructional Design: Learning ID Fast and Right by George Piskurich

The Mager Six-Pack by Roger Mager
- *Analyzing Performance Problems*
- *Preparing Instructional Objectives*
- *Measuring Instructional Results*
- *How to Turn Learners On ... Without turning Them Off*
- *Goal Analysis*
- *Making Instruction Work*

Developing Objectives

"Do we have to know this?"

"Is this going to be on the test?!?!"

At a very early age, we understood the concept of a learning objective. Unfortunately, training is sometimes designed and developed without taking the time to formally identify what the student is supposed to get out of the training! This can result in frustrated students (who don't know what they are supposed to be learning), inefficient training (that includes more than is necessary), or worse, ineffective training (that doesn't accomplish its goal).

Deciding on Your Objectives

During the analysis phase, you identified business problems or opportunities, identified underlying causes, and looked at potential solutions. It is now time to separate out the solutions you will implement that involve training and break them down into specific learning objectives.

According to the Big Dog's ISD Page, a learning objective is "A statement of what the learners will be expected to do when they have completed a specified course of instruction. It prescribes the conditions, behavior (action), and standard of task performance for the training setting."

Objectives help you decide what to include in the course, help the students understand what they will get and what will be expected of them, and help you evaluate the student and the course.

You may even want to create a hierarchy of objectives. For example, you may have course objectives, module objectives, and section objectives.

Pre-Requisites

In addition to determining what the objectives should be, you would also want to determine what they should <u>not</u> be. For a number of reasons, you will want to take the time to identify the knowledge, skills, and abilities you expect the learners to have before taking the course. This helps you:

- Decide what <u>not</u> to include in the course.
- Notify the student up front of the expectations.
- Set up pre-requisite training requirements, especially if you have a learning management system that can track such things.
- Develop your content to the right level of knowledge.

How Should They Be Phrased?

Elements

A strong learning objective will cover only one point, be focused on what the student will do, and will generally contain:

- A behavioral outcome.
- A condition.
- Success criteria or standard.

For example: Given a computer simulation, you will be able to use the XYZ scheduling software to create a schedule for all assembly-line workers that satisfies estimated production volume, requires no overtime, and complies with all labor and union laws.

Testability

A good learning objective is one that allows the student's mastery of it to be tested. In the world of e-learning, the relationship between objectives and testing might cause you to re-evaluate your objectives, especially if you are converting classroom training to e-learning. This is because your test options may be limited in an e-learning environment.

For example, you may have a classroom training objective that states: "Upon completion of this module, you will be able to discuss the differences between a Learning Management System and a Learning Content Management System. If the class is conducted via self-paced e-learning without an instructor, will they have the ability to truly <u>discuss</u> the difference? If your question options are limited to multiple choice questions, perhaps the best you can do is see if they can <u>recognize</u> the difference between an LMS and an LCMS. So then you have to make a decision: do you revise the objective or do you re-think your training format and testing options?

Other examples include:

- "Define" (perhaps to be replaced with "recognize the definition of")
- "List" (replaced with "select from a list")
- "Explain" (replaced with "identify")

Using scenarios and simulations may help you with more advanced objective types. For example, you may have an objective that asks your students to demonstrate a procedure or assemble a piece of equipment. If you can include an accurate online simulation, you may be able to keep those objectives, but stipulate that a simulation will be used.

Where Do They Go?

For an e-learning course, objectives generally go in one of three places. You'll want to decide which approach(es) to use.

- <u>Nowhere</u> – Sometimes the objectives are used only for the training developers and not presented to the student. Instead of formal objectives, you may want to use more benefits-driven marketing language to both "sell" and explain what is covered.

- <u>At the beginning of the course</u> – The complete list of objectives may appear on one of the screens in the overview or introduction of the course.

- <u>In the course catalog</u> – Depending upon how you are hosting your courses, it may be best for the students to be able to see the objectives in the course catalog or launch page so that they can decide if the course will meet their needs before committing to taking it.

Structuring the Content

Content Sequence and Flow

Once you have your objectives defined, you can begin to organize your content. During this part of the process, you will decide on the order and flow of the material. For example, you may want to organize the information in the order that it will come up on the job (such as a series of business, computer, or manufacturing processes), from the simple to the complex (such as scientific information or business theories), or from the general to the specific (such as employee orientation information about the industry, the company, then the department).

To help you with this sequencing, you may want to create a flow chart that helps you and your developers visualize the "big picture."

Course Hierarchy and Outline

With an e-learning course especially, you'll want to decide how the course can be broken down into "chunks."

First, you'll consider the question conceptually. You can determine how many "levels" in the course there will be. For example, will you have a course made of modules, which each contain lessons? You might also want guidelines about when to break something into its own module or lesson. You may even want to outline how much information should go on a single screen.

From there, you'll want to map out the actual content points to be included, in outline form. You are not writing the content at this stage, but you are outlining the courses, modules, and lessons.

You may even choose to outline the individual screens at this point, or leave that up to the developer. (Having a content list or outline for each particular screen will help your developers stay focused and succinct. Wordy or wandering e-learning gets expensive, so you'll want to make sure everyone knows exactly what they need to say – and don't need to say.)

Be sure to double-check that your outline contains enough information to meet the learning objectives, and doesn't contain information that is not needed to meet them.

Reusable Learning Objects

When developing an e-learning program, you'll want to decide if you want to structure your content in Reusable Learning Objects (or RLOs). According to e-Learning author William Horton, a 'learning object' is a chunk of electronic content that can be accessed individually and completely accomplishes a single learning goal and can prove it."

A learning object includes:

- The objective.
- The content needed to teach the objective.
- All related media elements.
- Pre-test questions.
- Embedded questions.
- Post-test questions.
- Any other elements related to that objective.

> **Alphabet Soup**
>
> RLO:
> Reusable Learning
> Object
>
> RIO:
> Reusable
> Information Object
>
> RCO:
> Reusable Content
> Object
>
> SCO:
> Sharable
> Courseware Object

A Reusable Learning Object is one that, as its name implies, is specifically structured to be used again in a different context: a different course, a different module, or even just presented in a different order based on who signed on to the course. There are three things that make a learning object reusable: intent, design, and technology.

Intent

Not all learning objects need to be re-used. You would plan to make learning objects reusable if you believed the information would be useful in a different setting, and, if so, could be presented in the exact same way. For example, you may have two groups who need information on dealing with customer conflict. But if one group deals with customers over the phone in a call center environment and the other group deals with customers in face-to-face meetings, each group would need a different "spin" on the content and reusability may not be a worthwhile goal.

Design

If you want an object to be reusable, it must be designed properly. For an object to truly be reusable, it must be able to stand alone. It cannot have references to material taught earlier or later. It must have clearly stated pre-requisite knowledge – pre-requisites that wouldn't change from one use to another. It would need all acronyms or new terminology spelled out the first time it was used in that object. It would not include any transitions, summaries, or application that includes information taught in another object.

Reusable learning objects would also need to be developed using the same style guidelines. Writing style, tone, typestyles, colors, graphics, and other design factors would need to be the same if you wanted to use an object in more than one place.

Technology

Certain programming considerations can be made to enhance the reusability of a learning object. Technically, an object can just be cut and pasted from one course to another, with no special programming required. But to ensure maximum flexibility, certain guidelines can be followed.

For example, you may have a two-hour course with several modules, pre-tests, module post-tests, course post-tests, a table of contents, and a searchable index. If you used the cut-and-paste method, you would have to go to each part of the course and find the related elements, hoping that you get them all. If you structure the technology right, all the elements are "tied together" behind the scenes and can be moved around as needed.

Object Repositories

To get the maximum benefit of reusability, you will want a place to store and catalog the objects so they can be found and re-used. This can be anything from a database, to a content management system, to an LCMS (Learning Content Management System).

Metadata

Metadata is data about the data. It is behind-the-scenes information that identifies and categorizes the object. Examples of metadata include author, date created or revised, and keywords – anything that would help others find, identify, and reuse that content. The object repository you use will determine how and where to manage your metadata.

SCORM Compliance

To ensure that your objects are as portable as possible, you will probably want to design them to industry standards, specifically SCORM. According to SCORM's creators, "The Sharable Content Object Reference Model (SCORM) aims to foster creation of reusable learning content as 'instructional objects' within a common technical framework for computer and Web-based learning." This reference model governs how learning objects should be structured and programmed so that it can work with other systems and programs. For more information on SCORM, go to www.adlnet.org.

Instructional Strategies

For each objective, you will want to outline the best way to present the information, to allow for practice and feedback, and to assess the student's performance.

Decisions about instructional strategies will generally drive the format you select for training (classroom, on-the-job, etc.) and, if e-learning is chosen, the selection of your authoring tool. However, in some cases the format and even authoring tool may be selected (or dictated) in advance, requiring it to drive the instructional strategies.

For example, you could pick a tool because you know you want a randomized bank of questions. (Select the tool based on instructional strategy.) Or you could specify only multiple-choice and true/false questions because that is all your tool can support. (Select instructional strategy based on the tool.)

Ideally, you would decide what the best way to train is, and then find the platform and tool to support that. Technology should *support* training decisions, not *drive* them. However, sometimes the reality of the situation wins out. You may already be locked into a certain tool or perhaps can't afford to buy or learn a tool that gives you all the options and features you really want. In these cases, you just have to weigh the benefits and the drawbacks and make the best decision that fits the training need and the business environment.

Presentation

Now that you have your objectives, you will need to decide the best way to present that information to the student. That decision can be made based on a number of factors such as:

- <u>Type of information</u> – Is it a fact, concept, attitude, procedure, behavior? Is it simple or complex? Is it likely to cause resistance or confusion?

- <u>What you want them to do with the information</u> – Do you want them to know something, believe something, and/or do something?

- <u>The level of mastery you want them to have</u> – Do you want them to be able to recall, comprehend, or apply a fact or concept? For a skill or procedure, do you want them to be able to perform it on their own or with guidance?

Refer to Benjamin Bloom's taxonomies for educational objectives for more information on these areas: the Cognitive (mental processes), Affective (attitudes, beliefs, and values), and Psychomotor (physical movement and coordination) domains. Big Dog's ISD Page has a great summary: http://www.sos.net/~donclark/hrd/bloom.html

Possible presentation strategies include:

- Video presentation (live or recorded)
- Audio presentation (live or recorded)
- Text narrative
- Lecture
- Question and answer
- Reflection
- On-the-job training
- Mentoring/coaching
- Scenarios
- Simulations
- Diagrams
- Exploratory activities
- Demonstrations
- Discussions
- Group activities
- Self-directed research
- Documents to be read
- Assignments

As you can probably imagine, some of these strategies would lend themselves very well to self-paced e-learning, some to synchronous learning, and some to classroom training. By selecting the best instructional strategies for each objective, you'll begin to create a picture of how your courses should be designed.

Practice

Wouldn't you hate to be the first patient for a medical student who just learned how to draw blood? What if she had only ever read about the procedure and maybe saw someone else do it, but had never actually tried it herself? Would you want your arm to be the first?

Effective training gives the students an opportunity to practice and receive feedback. For each objective in your course, you will want to determine the best way to provide that practice and feedback.

Some common practice options include:

- Fact checks (simple questions sprinkled throughout the presentation)
- Role-plays
- Games
- Scenario situations
- Simulated practices
- Hands-on practices
- Student demonstrations
- Group projects
- Written exercises

Think about how feedback can be provided – especially in a self-paced course. Could you provide standard feedback to everyone programmatically? Could you provide individual feedback programmatically? Would you need a person to review the student's work? Would you need a person to observe the student?

In addition, you'll want to decide what types of assistance or hints you might provide. For example, would the students have the benefit of a book or job aid? Could they try more than once? Could you provide hints or links back to where the content was originally taught?

Assessment

Remember that medical student drawing blood for the first time? You would probably want to know that she practiced, but you'd probably also want to know that someone with a high-level of knowledge in that area "signed off" on her ability to draw blood.

When making decisions about testing or assessments, you would think about many of the same issues as when you were looking at practices. You can use the same list of practice strategies as you can for assessment strategies. But with a formal assessment, you'll want to consider a few other factors as well:

- Do you want a pre-test and post-test?

- Do you want unit assessments, module assessments, and/or course assessments?

- Will you want to put security procedures in place to increase the integrity of the results?

- Do you want the students to have more than one try or receive assistance?

- Can the students refer to any materials or work together?

- Do you want the students to see the final score, the result of each question, the correct answer to each question, and/or the reason behind the correct answer? Do you want to see them to see this after each question or at the end of the test?

Outlining the Instructional Strategies

Once you have made your decisions, the information would be outlined either in a design document or lesson plan. You can use a simple table to capture your decisions or options for each objective.

Figure 6.1 Lesson Plan Grid

Go to the Resources page at **www.e-LearningUncovered.com** for a downloadable version of this grid.

Objective	Type of Information	Presentation	Practice	Assessment
Set up an out-of-office message in Outlook.	Procedure	Demonstration (live or simulated) with narrative text (written or presented) to provide context.	Hands-on practice, either simulated or in a live system, with the ability to reference the procedure if needed, and feedback for each step (either system generated or provided by an instructor).	Hands-on practice in a real or simulated environment without reference to the procedure. Correct or incorrect feedback provided, but without explanation or assistance.

Selecting the Best Format

It may feel like you decided to do e-learning all the way back in Chapter 1 when reviewing the advantages and disadvantages. But the formal approach has you hold off on your decision until this point. Using this method helps you ensure that the technology is supporting the training, and not vice-versa.

As you review your list of instructional strategies, make some determinations about what the best format would be.

Classroom or Distance; Instructor or Self-Paced

Based on everything you have already decided, it should now become clear whether certain objectives can best be met in a classroom, or if the students can do it on their own. Even if they can do it on their own, you'll have a good idea as to whether an instructor would need to be involved, or if it can truly be a stand-alone, self-paced course. When making this decision, look not only at your instructional strategies, but also your business environment such as budget, schedule, and volume. You may find that one format is better for instructional design reasons, but another format is better for business reasons.

Blended Learning: the Best of Both Worlds

You may find that each format has some value based on the business situation. For example:

- An e-learning format is great for presenting the factual information on a new product being released by your company, but not as good for the more subjective elements such what objections might be presented by the customer and how to handle them.
- You are able to provide background information and demonstrate the technique for a mechanical procedure through online video and electronic support documents, but the students must really use the actual equipment for practice and assessment.

In these situations, you may want a blended approach and use both e-learning and a more traditional form such as classroom or on-the-job training. The e-learning portion could be completed as pre-work and then the classroom used for discussion, application, practice, and assessment.

Special e-Learning Considerations

Standards and Compliance

The design phase is the perfect time to decide if you want or need your courses or other e-learning systems to comply with any industry standards and guidelines.

SCORM/AICC Compliance

While SCORM governs the development of Reusable Learning Objects, it also provides guidelines for how courses and Learning Management Systems work together. AICC is a similar industry standard designed to increase interoperability between systems. It stands for Aviation Industry CBT Committee and it was one of the early e-learning standards. While it is not as common as SCORM, it is still a reliable standard and there are many authoring tools and LMSs that are AICC complaint.

Section 508 Compliance

Section 508 is a provision in the Americans with Disabilities Act that provides guidelines for all Federal government agencies to ensure their electronic communication is accessible to those with disabilities. e-Learning falls under the category of electronic communication.

> *If you want to make sure your courses are accessible to those with disabilities, review the guidelines for compliance with Section 508 of the Rehabilitation Act.*
>
> *www.section508.gov*

You may want your courses to be Section 508 compliant for one of two reasons:

- You are a Federal government agency or are creating courses for a Federal government agency and therefore must be Section 508 compliant.
- You are not required to comply but you know you have people with disabilities in your target audience and you want to use the Section 508 provisions as a guideline to make sure your courses are accessible.

115

The guidelines ensure compatibility with assistive devices for people with visual, auditory, or motor skills issues. Assistive devices include equipment such as a screen reader for someone who can't see the screen, or mouse alternatives such as a breathing device that controls the on-screen pointer for someone who cannot use a mouse.

There are also guidelines to make sure the course is not reliant on common e-learning elements that cannot be used by everyone. For example, if there is audio in a course, you want to make sure there is a text alternative for those with hearing disabilities. You would want keyboard alternatives for any action requiring the mouse for those with motor skills issues that prevent them from using a mouse, or for someone with visual restrictions who cannot see what the mouse needs to do on-screen.

Even if you do not need/choose to make your courses Section 508 compliant, consider those in your target audience with disabilities that may impact how they experience the course. Decide on a strategy to ensure they get equal access to the training opportunities.

For more information about Section 508 compliance, go to www.section508.gov.

Summary

Now you know very clearly what needs to be taught (your objectives, that is), the overall structure of the course, some high-level strategies for presentation, practice, and assessment, and some ideas about the best format to use. As you continue through the design phase, you will add even more detail to this plan. Chapter 7 will describe how to translate your instructional plan into specific course features and functions.

7

The Design Phase: Course Features and Functions

By this point in the process, you now have a good idea about who your audience is, what their environment is, what you need to teach them, and some broad instructional strategies to get you there. Now it is time to translate all of that information into the specific elements to be used in your courses.

During this part of the design phase, you will make and document decisions about how to handle everything from questions and interactions to interface design and use of media. These decisions will be collected in your design document and used by the people actually developing the courses.

Testing and Assessments

One of the most commonly cited advantages of moving to an e-learning platform is the ability to provide tests, practice, and feedback. With all the benefits of online testing come a number of different design choices. When making design decisions and actually constructing your questions, you'll want to first understand your goals, then create a strategy, and, finally, build and evaluate the questions.

Determining Your Testing Goals

There are many variables that go into the design and development of questions in an e-learning course. But before you make these decisions, it is important to first understand why you want to include testing. Once you are clear on your goals, the decisions become easier.

Use the following list to identify why you want to include testing. (Notice that "because I can" is not one of the options!) For any given course, more than one of these reasons may apply.

- Interaction – You want to use questions as a way to keep students engaged and involved.

- Self-awareness – You want the student to know, for their own benefit, how they are doing: This can help them decide for themselves if they need to go back and re-study any of the information.

- Remediation and correction – You want to provide the student feedback on their mastery of the material and re-direct them as needed.

- Reinforcement – You want to make sure a certain teaching point is not only learned, but also remembered, so you use a question as a way to reinforce the information.

- Course direction – You want to create customized learning paths for each student based on what they already know.

- Course evaluation – You want to determine if the course truly taught what it was supposed to teach.

- Student evaluation – You want to know if the student knows what you want him or her to know.

- Certification – You want to be 100% sure a student knows what you want him or her to know, and you want to be able to document it.

Creating a Testing Strategy

Once you understand the goals of your testing, you can move forward with creating a testing strategy. This includes a number of one-time decisions about how questions will be structured, written, programmed, and presented.

Question Types

The types of questions you use would ideally be driven by the type of content you have and the specific objectives. However, sometimes your question types may be dictated by the authoring tool you are using or by whether or not you have an instructor available to you. Remember also that you can use a blended strategy for testing where the student learns the information through e-learning but then is tested in a classroom or work setting by a peer, supervisor, or instructor.

Multiple Choice

Multiple-choice questions are by far the most common in e-learning, whether it is the most appropriate format or not. These question types are best for facts, concepts, and even applications – if developed in a scenario format.

Which of the following statements is the best example of focusing on a job-related concern?

- A. Do you have any children?
- B. Do you have reliable child care arrangements for your children?
- C. Promptness is important to this job. Will you be able to be on time every day?
- D. Do your kids make you late to work a lot?

Design/programming decisions you'll need to make about multiple-choice questions include:

- Will there be only one right answer or multiple right answers?
- How many options can you have? Does it have to be the same for every question?
- How will the options be presented? Check boxes, radio buttons, drop-down menu, or hot spot?

When developing multiple-choice questions, keep these tips in mind:

- Use realistic distracters (the "wrong" answers).
- If you are using randomized options, do not put letters next to the options or in the remediation. When appropriate, use "all of these" or "none of these" instead of "all of the above" or "none of the above" so options can be put anywhere on the screen.

- If you are using the word "not" in the question, emphasize that word with bolding, underlining, etc., so the student doesn't accidentally skim over it. For example: Which of the following situations is NOT an example of ..."

- If students can pick more than one correct answer, be sure to tell them.

True/False

Many designers do not like true/false questions because they are too easy to guess. Developers often like them because they are easy to write. True/false questions should be saved for straight-forward factual information with little room for interpretation, such as policies and procedures.

> It is appropriate to ask an applicant what year he or she graduated from high school.
>
> ○ True
> ○ False

When developing true/false questions, keep these tips in mind:

- Avoid using negative statements to be evaluated. For example: "Decide if the following statement is true or false. New York City is not the capital of the state of New York." When a negative statement is true, someone might be misled into selecting false.

- Be careful not to accidentally put a question mark at the end of the statement being evaluated.

Matching

Matching questions can be programmed many ways in an e-learning course, but all have the student pair up two different facts, concepts, or even pictures. These questions work well with terminology, classifications, or even software commands.

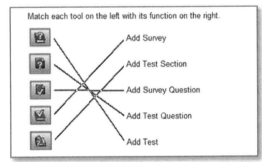

Design/programming decisions you'll need to make about matching questions include:

- Can you use one option more than once?

- Can you have an option that is not used at all?

- Can you include graphics for half of each pair?

- How will the question function? Click on an option and then its match, type in a letter, drag an imaginary line, or drag an image?

When developing matching questions, keep these tips in mind:

- Be sure to include clear directions about how to operate the question.

- Most students will assume there is a one-to-one match between the options, so if an option can be used more than once or if there will be an option left over, be sure to point that out.

Fill-in-the-blank

A fill-in-the-blank question requires a higher level of mastery from the students because they need to remember the answer on their own, rather than just  recognize it in a list. In a truly self-paced environment, grading can be challenging if there are different ways to spell or format the answer.

For example, could the correct answer take the singular or plural form? Are there different spellings of the word (such as color and colour)? If the correct answer is a time or date, might some students format the answer differently than others (especially if they are from different parts of the world)?

Design/programming decisions you'll need to make about fill-in-the-blank questions include:

- Can more than one answer be considered correct? How many maximum?

- Can you have more than one blank per question?

When developing fill-in-the-blank questions, keep these tips in mind:

- Make all blanks equal in length so it doesn't give away any clues to the answer.

- Brainstorm all the possible answers and different ways to spell, format, or phrase the answer. If there are too many options, consider a different question type.

- Consider whether you want to accept the correct answer even if it is spelled incorrectly. (Are you judging whether they know the answer, whether they can spell the answer, or both?)

- Decide if you want the answer to be case-sensitive.

Short Answer/Essay

Short answer and essay questions require a subjective evaluation, and therefore the involvement of an instructor. If that is an option for you, you can include this type of question when you want to test a higher-level understanding of the material.

Drag-and-Drop

With a drag-and-drop question, you ask the student to use the mouse to move some element to a certain part of the screen. There are many variations this question type can take, including labeling parts of a diagram, putting steps in order, or putting information into categories.

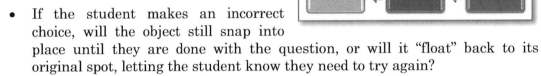

Design decisions you'll need to make about drag-and-drop questions include:

- If the student makes an incorrect choice, will the object still snap into place until they are done with the question, or will it "float" back to its original spot, letting the student know they need to try again?

- Will there be items that are not used in the answer?

When developing matching questions, keep these tips in mind:

- Try to make the "drop spots" bigger than the item being dragged. This makes sure you are testing the students' knowledge and not their mouse skills.

- Make sure the graphics and the technology don't overwhelm the student. The question should be easy to read and easy to use.

- Provide very clear instructions. If working with a novice audience, just asking them to drag the items on the left and drop it in the correct sequence on the right may not be adequate – you'll probably want to explain how to drag and how to drop.

Simulation

The word "simulation" is defined differently by different people in the world of e-learning. For this discussion, simulation means a simulated environment for a process, software usage, or equipment usage. For example, in a course on math, you may be asked to perform calculations on a simulated on-screen calculator. In a retail course, you may be asked to ring-up a sale on a simulated cash register. In a course on desktop software, you may be given a simulated environment of the software and be asked to perform a procedure.

These simulations can be very effective as they are job-oriented and performance-focused. They are also more expensive to create and maintain.

There are also business simulations which can often be considered an elaborate version of one of the other question types. For example, you may have a role-play scenario about how to handle a conflict situation. Different characters are presented and you are asked what you would say in the given situation. This is an advanced form of a multiple-choice question.

Quiz Games

There are many programs available that allow you to create game-like quizzes. Many of these games operate like popular game shows or board games. These games can be a good choice if you need lots of repetition and drilling to make sure your audience truly remembers the information. Games can also be a nice touch when you expect your audience has low motivation for the subject or a low attention span.

When developing questions for games, keep these tips in mind:

- Make sure your instructions are clear. Be careful assuming your students will already know how to play even a well-known board game or game show format – especially if you have a global audience.

- Avoid games when creating a formal assessment or certification. When you want to rely 100% on the results of a test, keep it simple.

- Make sure the information lends itself to a game format. Don't let the "coolness" of the game overpower what you are trying to accomplish.

- Avoid games when you have a direct, straight-forward audience who is self-motivated and with limited time available. This group may find the games distracting or consider them a waste of time.

Placement

Based on your testing goals, you may want pre-tests, post-tests, and/or individual questions embedded throughout the content.

Pre-tests

Pre-tests are generally used in two situations: when you want to judge the effectiveness of the course (comparing "before" knowledge to "after" knowledge) or when you want a custom learning path for the student. There are several options for using a pre-test for custom learning paths.

- Test results automatically pull up only the content the student has not mastered, with credit given for the rest of the material.

- Test results give credit for the material mastered and suggest a path, but the student can take the entire course, if desired.
- Test results provide a suggestion for the learner to use as they see fit. There is no credit given and all content is available.

Post-Tests

Post-tests can be included at the end of each lesson, module, course, or even some combination of these. Generally, these tests are scored and tracked. Based on your testing goals, you will want to decide when the tests are given and how they will be scored. For example, you may want a post-test at the end of each lesson for reinforcement and for the student to decide if he or she is ready to move on. Then you may include a scored and tracked post-test at the end of the entire course that you use for certification purposes.

You'll also want to decide if you want the test to reside within the course or outside of the course. In some LMS systems, the test is considered a separate learning event.

Embedded Questions

Most courses have questions sprinkled throughout the content, perhaps every 5 to 10 screens. Generally, these questions are for practice, reinforcement, remediation, and to keep the student engaged. They are usually not tracked and are most often included just for the benefit of the student.

Number of questions

Some people choose to specify how many questions will be delivered per learning objective. For example, you may say you want two questions per objective in both the pre-test and the post-test. Others instead prefer to let the objective dictate the number of questions needed, as not all objectives are created equal. You will also want to decide if you would use the same questions in the pre-test and post-test, or if you would create separate versions of the questions.

Remediation

The term remediation can be used broadly to describe any feedback given to a student during a practice or test exercise. Technically, it means correcting a fault. Based on your testing goals, there are a number of ways to handle remediation and other student guidance for test and quiz questions. Several options are listed below, from least remediation to most remediation.

End-of-Test Remediation

Remediation can be provided as each question is answered, or in a summary report given at the end of the test. In general, remediation is saved for the end in formal assessments and certifications.

- <u>Final score only</u> – When you need an extremely reliable test, you may choose to show the student only the final score at the end. This keeps them from simply writing down the answers so they can re-take the quiz. It also minimizes sharing of answers. However, it does not provide any real feedback or guidance to the student.

- <u>Right/wrong indication</u> – The next level would be to show the final score at the end and let them know which questions they did or didn't get right – but without showing them the answers. This again keeps the integrity of your test high, and at least lets the student know what areas they missed.

- <u>Answers provided for questions missed</u> – When you want to provide the student with some level of feedback, you may choose to display only the questions they got wrong, along with the correct answer. This increases the remediation for the student, but does allow them to copy down or share that information. Another downside is that they don't receive confirmation of the correct answer if they merely guessed and got it right.

- <u>Answers provided for all questions at the end of the test</u> – Providing answers to all of the questions gives useful direction to the student for areas needing improvement and reinforcement for those questions answered correctly. However, such a summary list would be easy to use when re-taking the test or to share with other students.

Per-Question Remediation

When you want your student to learn from each question, as well as be assessed by it, you may choose to provide remediation when they finish each and every question. Your options may be limited by your authoring tool.

- <u>Standard for the whole course</u> – Some systems will allow you to provide remediation for each question, but there can only be one "correct" message and one "incorrect" message for the entire course. This lets the student know if they got the answer right or wrong.

- <u>Question-specific remediation without explanation</u> – This indicates whether or not the student got the answer right, and also gives what the right answer is, but with no explanation as to why.

- <u>Question-specific remediation with explanation</u> – In addition to indicating whether or not the student got the question right and what the right answer was, you may want to include an explanation that provides details on why the answer is correct. With this level of remediation, they see the same answer whether they got it right or wrong.

- <u>Per correct or incorrect response</u> – This is a slight variation on the previous method, but you can have two possible messages: one if the student answered correctly, and one if they didn't.

- <u>Per-option remediation</u> – This is the most detailed form of remediation where there is a separate message displayed based on which individual option the student selected such as one message if they guessed "a" and a different message if they guessed "b", even through both are wrong. This allows you to provide more tailored feedback by addressing what was right or wrong about the specific choice the student made.

Other options

- <u>More than one attempt allowed</u> – Based on your programming or authoring tool, you may be able to determine the number of attempts a student can have for a certain question before being given the answer or being moved on to the next question. This is generally not done with formal assessments but is done when your goal is to give the student the opportunity to explore and remember.

- <u>Hints and other help</u> – When the questioning is for reinforcement, you can provide assistance to the students if they are struggling. Hints can take the form of a pop-up window that provides relevant text from the course, a link back to where that content was taught (make sure you provide a link to take them back to the question), access to a job aid or reference guide, or some sort of visual clue such as an arrow or box highlighting the portion of the screen learners should be looking at (used often with diagrams or computer simulations).

- <u>Navigation</u> – You can also set up a relationship between success on a question and remediation. For example, you can choose to set navigation so the students can't move on until a question is answered correctly. You could set a test so the students are automatically taken back to the parts of the course that covers what they missed. You could also provide the students with links to the material for any questions missed and they can choose if they want to go back and review it again. Finally, for compliance or mandated courses, you may want to prevent access to the final test until a student completes all elements of the course.

Design Tips for Remediation

- <u>Purpose</u> – with all of these options available to you, stay true to your purpose. Review your objectives, what you know about your audience, and your goals for testing when making all of these decisions. Don't let the features and options overpower what you are trying to do.

- Courtesy – Use respectful, but not patronizing, language when providing feedback on incorrect answers.

- Color-coding – Be careful about using only color to indicate the right or wrong answer. 8% of men have some sort of color blindness. If you want to use red and green to reinforce, that is fine – just make sure color is not the ONLY indicator. For example, a red "x" and a green checkmark would work well since the color is not critical to getting the message. However, coloring the connecting lines either green or red on a matching exercise would not be understood by someone with red-green color blindness.

- Usefulness – If you are going to take the time and effort to script out remediation for each question or even each option, make sure you are providing valuable insight for the student. If there is a visual display of the right answer (such as the correct answer being bolded) and your text remediation just says the same thing in written form, you are probably wasting development time. Either add something to the message, or rely just on the visual indicators.

Randomization

If you are concerned about the integrity of your test, you may want to include some randomization options – such as mixing up the order of the questions or using different questions each time. This is generally done in two situations: (1) You want to make sure that if students need to re-take the test, they are truly being re-tested on the content, rather than being re-tested on whether they remember what the right and wrong answers were the first time around. (2) You feel there is a reasonable chance the students will share answers and you want to minimize that as much as possible. Common randomization options are listed below, from simplest to most complex:

- Order of options – With this type of randomization, all of the same questions appear for each student each time one of them takes the test. However, each time a question appears, the options are in a different order. For example, on a multiple-choice question the correct answer might be the first choice for one student and the second choice for another student. This at least keeps the student from being able to quickly write down the letter of the correct answer. Sharing and note-taking can still occur, but at least the people involved would need to write down the correct concept and not just a letter.

- Order of questions – Another method that provides similar benefits is to have the same questions appear for everyone, but have them appear in a different order. Again, this makes it a little more challenging to make notes or share answers.

- <u>Questions pulled from a question bank</u> – A higher level of security is created when you have different questions appear for each person, or each time the same person takes a quiz. To do this, you would create more questions than will be used, and the course creates a unique quiz for each person. For example, you may create 20 questions but each person only gets 10. This reduces the effectiveness of note-taking and sharing. If the questions are being pulled randomly, it isn't possible to guarantee that a question from each objective will be pulled. As a result, the student might be double-tested on one objective, and not tested on others.

- <u>Questions pulled per objective from a bank</u> – A way to guarantee all objectives are met with a question bank is to use programming that pulls at least one question for each objective. Doing this requires objectives to be identified, several questions to be developed for each objective, those questions to be labeled by objective behind the scenes, and the test engine to be able to pull one (or two, three, etc.) from each objective to create the test. This is one of the most secure self-paced testing methods you can use while still guaranteeing all objectives are tested. This method also requires the most logic to be programmed into your system or be built-in to your authoring tool.

Special Note: When looking at authoring tools, talking to development vendors, or working with your own development team, make sure you are clear about what type of randomization you want. If you use the term "randomized bank of questions," different people may have different interpretations of what that means. Instead, be specific.

Other Options

Depending on your tool, there are a number of options for your testing strategy. Review what it is you are trying to accomplish and consider any customization to help you meet those objectives. Some other options include:

- Allowing partial credit for any question that requires knowledge of several pieces of information (such as a multiple-choice question with more than one correct answer or a matching question).

- Putting one question on a screen or having all questions on one scrolling screen.

- Weighing some questions more heavily than others in the overall score.

- Setting a time limit to answer the questions. (Be careful about using this option as technical difficulties, physical disabilities, language barriers, or learning disabilities may all affect how long it takes a person to take a test.)

- Incorporating media elements into the question (audio, video, or graphics).

The Question Creation Process

Writing <u>good</u> questions can easily be the most time-consuming part of building your content. (Ineffective questions can be written very quickly!) To make sure you stay on track, be sure to review your objectives carefully and always use them as your guide.

The Question Outline List

One way to help you stay focused is to forget about the actual questions themselves. Instead, think about the point you want to test or reinforce. Review your objectives (and your content if it already exists) and ask yourself the following questions:

- If a student walked away knowing only one thing, what should it be?
- Six months after taking the course, when the student is on the job on some Tuesday afternoon, what will be the most important things for him or her to remember?
- What information has no room for error?
- What information is likely to cause the most trouble if the student forgets or misunderstands it?
- What information is likely to create the greatest benefits if the student implements it correctly?

Use these questions to come up with a list of your most critical teaching points.

Figure 7.1 Question Outline List

Go to the Resources page at **www.e-LearningUncovered.com** for a downloadable version of this list.

Objective: Enter an item into the new product database.	
Fact	**Question**
Items will have new item numbers, with 6 digits instead of 5.	
A "7" at the beginning of the item number means it is a corporate brand item.	
There are separate fields for suggested retail price and our actual price.	
New items need to be entered by noon on Wednesday to be sent to the stores in the weekly update.	

From there, turn each of these points into a question that fully tests or reinforces the point. This will help you make sure you aren't testing irrelevant information just because it makes an easy question, and ensures your tests are practical and application-based.

The Fact-Idea-Question List

Another way to generate questions is to take the facts generated in Figure 7.1 and then focus on ideas – rather than the question.

Figure 7.2 Fact-Idea-Question List
Go to the Resources page at **www.e-LearningUncovered.com** for a downloadable version of this list.

Objective: Enter an item into the new product database.		
Fact	**Idea**	**Question**
New items need to be entered by noon on Wednesday to be sent to the stores in the weekly update.	Drop-down list with time and day. Calendar/Clock where they have to click the right day and time.	

From there, turn each of these ideas into a question that fully tests or reinforces the point. Once the ideas are generated, you could also delegate question-writing to someone else.

Common Mistakes with e-Learning Questions

The ability to write good questions shouldn't be much different for e-learning than for traditional instruction. So why then, are there so many bad tests out there? Perhaps it is because written tests are not often used in classrooms outside academia. Therefore, experienced instructional designers and trainers may not have much experience creating questions in any training format – e-learning or otherwise.

Here are some common mistakes you'll want to avoid:

Questions don't test the most important information.

Too often, test questions are built based on what is easy to test. Simple, factual material is the easiest information to create a test question around. However, these factual points may just be supplemental information rather than the important points that deserve reinforcement and assessment.

Solution: Review your objectives and create a question outline first. Then develop your questions from that list.

Questions don't fully test the objective.

Some tests provide just one or two simple questions about single facts in a lesson. Knowing the answer to those one or two questions does not mean the student has fully achieved the objective.

Solution: Review your objectives and create a teaching point list first. Then develop your questions from that list.

Directions are unclear.

Whether you are using a simple multiple-choice question or a more elaborate drag-and-drop or simulation question, the student could be paralyzed by not

---

Avoiding Answer Give-Aways

Be careful when using "always" or "never" in a true/false question. Savvy test takers know that "false" is the safe guess in those cases.

If you are going to use "none of the above" or "all of the above" in a multiple-choice question, be sure to use these as distracters occasionally. Savvy test takers know that often they are only included when they are the right answer, making them a good guess.

Try to have all the options a similar length. When one option is much longer than the others, savvy test takers know it's a safe bet.

Use parallel construction for your options when asking students to complete a sentence in a multiple-choice format. Savvy test takers know to look for inconsistencies in subject-verb agreement, singular vs. plural, or "a" vs. "an" when deciding which option to choose.

---

understanding how to operate the question. For example, with a multiple-choice question, do they click on the right response or type in a letter? Can they select more than one correct option? Your questions should judge their knowledge of the information, not their ability to figure out how the question works.

Solution: Remember the skill level of your audience when constructing questions and think like a true beginner when writing instructions for them.

Questions have "clues" about the correct answer.

Experienced test-takers (and test-avoiders) have learned over time how to increase their odds when guessing at a question.

Solution: Use the tips in the box to the right to make sure you aren't helping out the guessers.

Questions don't match the content.

Believe it or not, there are tests out there that test content not covered in the material or content covered in a different module. A more subtle, but just as dangerous, problem is questions that test content to a degree not covered in the module.

For example, in a class on hiring discrimination, one module covered what the law says about what is considered discrimination. The test asks what interview questions are legal and illegal. Unfortunately, the module never translated the discrimination law to the types of questions that were or were not appropriate in an interview.

Solution: Have clearly defined objectives and questions before you develop your content. Have a full review of the course done by someone not involved in the development process.

Questions have unclear answers.

Because not everything in the world is black and white, it can be challenging to create every objective multiple-choice and true/false questions for every type of content – and, yet, that is what some developers try to do. Because of this, some questions are, well, questionable! There may be incorrect options that really are correct in the right situation. And yet, because it wasn't what was taught in the class, the option is deemed incorrect. Because there may not be an instructor to clarify the answers, you can be causing confusion in the minds of the learner and inadvertently labeling a positive idea as really being negative.

Solution: Try to argue with your own questions to see if there might be a different perspective. Make sure you aren't marking something as incorrect just because it is not the focus of your lesson.

Interactions

There is a difference between training and a keynote speech. The first is generally a two-way, back-and-forth exchange and the second is one-way communication. Similarly, there is a difference between e-learning and e-reading! Effective e-learning provides interaction for the student while e-reading is a more passive activity.

Just as a classroom training session can be made more effective by questions, activities, games, and discussions, so can your e-learning.

Reasons for Interaction

As with any element of the design phase, you'll want to start out by understanding your purpose. Games, activities, and interactions can be used for:

- Reinforcement understanding.
- Application of the material.
- Retention.
- Practice.
- Motivation to learn.
- Fun.

Types of Interactions

Based on what you are trying to accomplish, there are many, many options at your disposal.

Offline Activities

Offline activities are any activities that do not involve the course. While the instructions and the assignment may reside in the course, the students would actually perform the activity outside of the course. This opens up a number of additional options for you, but does not provide any feedback to the students unless the work is submitted to an instructor. Options might include:

- Reflection questions (For example: "Think about the best teacher you ever had and jot down some of the things you liked best about him or her. Then review the list and see how many of the same qualities hold true for a good supervisor.")

- Internet research (Ask the student to look up the origin of the Section 508 guidelines for e-learning.)

- Software application assignments (Provide the files and instructions for students to perform a software task, but then have them complete the task on their own version of the software, instead of in the course itself.)

- Traditional homework assignments and projects (If appropriate, you can assign anything you might assign in a classroom environment.)

Collaborative Activities

Collaborative activities require the involvement of an instructor, a mentor, and/or other class members. These activities require that other students are going through the same course at the same time, but they allow for the type of discussion and feedback that can be so useful in a classroom environment. Examples include:

- Threaded discussions/forums
- E-mail discussions
- Group projects
- Surveys and polls

Simple Online Activities (Asynchronous)

- Reinforcement questions (multiple-choice, matching, drag-and-drop)
- Screen management (any interaction that requires student involvement to display on-screen information, such as rollovers and pop-ups)
- Situational scenarios (more elaborate forms of questions where the fact or concept is put in a job-specific context and the student has to make decisions about a realistic situation based on the course content)

Advanced Online Activities (Asynchronous)

Advanced activities include simulations and games, both discussed earlier in the chapter.

Tips for Designing Interactions

- Start with a list of points to be reinforced. Interactions can be the most time-consuming and expensive part of e-learning development – so make sure you have a point!! You can use the same list you created for your questions. If they are worth testing, they are worth reinforcing.
- Consider some sort of interaction every 5 to 7 screens.
- Make instructions clear.
- Ensure your training objective is met. Don't get too carried away with the fun factor.
- Consider the "shelf-life" of the material before designing an interaction. Information that might need to be updated periodically may be a good choice for a simple question rather than an elaborate simulation – to keep maintenance costs down.

Media

Your media choices will be made based on a combination of technical factors, audience factors, and learning issues.

Graphics and Animations

Graphics and animations in an e-learning course can either be decorative or informative. Because of the file size and the time needed to find, make, or prepare them for your course, you may want to limit yourself to those instructional in nature. When done properly, a graphic can be a great way to communicate a lot of information in a very small space. They can also set a tone or evoke an emotion.

You may want to designate a certain style for the graphics overall, based on the audience, the mood, etc. For example, will you be using stock photography, actual photos from the work environment, clip art, cartoons, or custom graphics – even custom-created characters?

If there are limits on file size, pixel size, or file format, be sure to define those at this stage of the project.

Audio

Whether or not to include audio in your e-learning course can turn into a great debate. There are pros and cons to both sides and many ways to approach it.

Pros and Cons of Using Audio

Reasons to use audio include:

- Reinforcement and retention – When information is presented using several different senses or experiences, retention is improved.
- Language and literacy barriers – Some students who may struggle with a text-based course may do better with audio information.
- An engaging experience – The addition of media such as audio can mean a richer experience for some students.

Reasons to avoid using (or at least relying on) audio include:

- <u>Technology restrictions</u> – The audience may not have speakers or head phones and sound cards.

- <u>Budget limitations</u> – Professional-sounding audio can be expensive to produce and expensive to maintain when there are changes.

- <u>Environment restrictions</u> – Background noise in the students' environment could interfere with them listening to the course, or the audio in the course could interfere with what is going on in the background.

- <u>Disability issues</u> – A portion of your audience may have hearing impairments.

Audio-Optional

Because there are significant pros and cons to the audio issue, many designers build courses that are audio-optional. This means the course can be played with audio, but doesn't require it.

This can be accomplished in several ways:

- Having the audio match the on-screen text exactly.

- Having a full-text version of the course available (perhaps by including a link to a .pdf document with the text) or having an on-screen transcript that can be turned on and off.

- Providing two separate versions of the course: one with audio and one without.

- Using audio to provide the full information and use summary bullet points on-screen. (Use caution with this method because you don't want the non-audio user to miss out on any important information).

Audio Controls

To give the student the most flexibility, you may want to consider including an audio on/off selector, volume control within the course window, and pause, stop, and replay buttons.

Video

Video can be a great option when you want to demonstrate a procedure or to add a human touch to your presentation. However, video can be very expensive to develop and has large file sizes, especially if the playback quality of the video is important.

The same pros and cons apply to video as were previously discussed in the audio section. You are adding the visual element, so you will also want to consider the monitor quality and size and any visual impairments of your audience members when choosing video.

Interface and Navigation

Have you ever gotten lost in a Website and couldn't figure out how to get back where you came from? Have you ever suffered through a presentation that used every single color, font, and animation available? In each of these cases, you've suffered from poor design – either in form or in function.

The interface design for your e-learning course includes the graphic design elements, the special features and functions, and the navigation. It is the structure that houses the content. Making good choices about your interface design and navigation can mean the difference between an enjoyable, effective learning session and a frustrating waste of time.

When thinking about interface design, consider each word individually.

> Interface: You are creating the interface between the students and the content. The students are trying to retrieve information and they "operate" the interface to do so. Therefore, your interface design should be structured, logical, consistent, and orderly, so the students know where they are and what they should do to get the results they want.

> Design: For the vast majority of your users, the e-learning course will be a visual experience. Therefore, the course should be designed in a visually pleasing way that sets the right tone and supports the message without interfering with it.

Graphic Design

In a perfect world, every e-learning development team will be able to work with a professional graphic artist for their course design. However, this task often falls to those without formal training or experience. Fortunately, effective e-learning interface design is very similar to effective Website design.

While it is impossible to cover everything you might need to know about good graphic design, here are a few highlights to make sure you are on the right track.

Fonts

- Never sacrifice legibility for creativity.

- Pick no more than three fonts or font styles for your course. Use one for headings, one for text, and one for special attention such as titles, warnings, etc.

Have your interface design approved by your marketing department and anyone else who might have strong preferences about fonts, colors, and logo usage.

- Make sure your text font is easy to read. If you can, stay with text between 10 and 12 points. Select a simple font such as Verdana.

- Apply no more than one (maybe two) formatting styles to any element. Bold, italic, underlined, colored, shadowed type is overkill!

Colors

- Keep it simple. Select a neutral background color and two accent colors. Use the accent colors for headings, borders, graphs, etc. A unified color scheme makes your work look more professional.

- Have your on-screen text black or dark blue if it appears on a light background or white or off-white if it is on a dark background. Make sure there is enough contrast between the text and the background so it can be read clearly. (Again, never sacrifice legibility for creativity.)

- Avoid background patterns. They cause too much eye strain.

Page Layout

- You will probably want to create several page layouts to be used for different screen types. For example, you may want one design for module titles, another for text with a graphic, one for a large graphic with little or no text, one for a lot of text without a graphic, etc.

- Keep your design clean and simple. Provide for adequate page margins as well as space between on-screen elements (such as the text and a graph). In most cases, one graphic per screen is enough.

- When creating your overall interface design (header, footer, menu, etc.), be sure to use space-efficient elements so you have enough "real estate" on the page to fit a sufficient amount of content.

Buttons

- Label all buttons with text so there is no question what they are for.

- When possible, use Web standards for buttons that provide a different look when a button is active or inactive, rolled over, or clicked.

- Don't be afraid to have a little fun with the buttons. You have some room to be creative here as long as there is no question what the buttons are for.

Questions to make sure you haven't made a major design blunder.

Can I read everything?

If I had to look at this for an hour straight, would it give me a headache?

Can I tell what everything is for?

Does it scream "professionalism" or "lemonade stand"?

Navigation Options

"Where am I?" "Are we there yet?" "I think I'm lost." "How do I get out of here?" No, these aren't just phrases heard from the kids in the back seat of the car on a long road trip. These are things your students might be thinking in terms of how to move around the course. Setting up clear and purposeful navigation will help your students get the right information.

Fixed vs. Flexible Navigation

You'll want to start by making some fundamental decisions about who is in control. And once again, go back to your objectives, business need, and audience analysis to make that decision.

Flexible navigation allows the students to move freely around the course, taking only the sections they want, in the order they want. This method is best used when you have an audience who is motivated, one who can make sound judgments about what they need to learn, or information that is helpful but not required.

Forced navigation requires the students complete the course in a pre-set format, without the ability to move around. This method is best when you have an audience that has to take the training but doesn't really want to, one that doesn't have a good grasp of what they do or don't need to learn, or mandated information.

You can create variations and hybrids of these two models. For example:

- You can loosen up fixed navigation by requiring a set path through the course until it is completed and passed, but then "releasing" the navigation so the student can move around freely for review, refresher, performance support, etc.

- You can tighten fixed navigation by requiring that every element on a page be completed (such as the audio playing completely, all rollovers or hot spots accessed, etc.) before the student can select the Next button.

Choose your strategy carefully. Too much control given to a student in the wrong situation can result in very little learning taking place. Too much control taken from a student who can work independently can be very frustrating and can take longer than it needs to.

Progress and Location Indicators

Menu Options

Even if the student will not have control of the navigation, it might still be useful for the students to see a menu for the course so they will know what to expect. If the students do have control, then the menu is the tool that allows them to move freely around the course.

Your best choice is to have the menu just one click away at all times. You can use a button in the interface or even a drop-down box. Another helpful option is to include a button that allows the student to return to the beginning of the course or module, if desired.

Try to avoid going more than three levels deep with menu options. For example, you may have a course made up of modules (level 1). The modules are comprised of lessons (level 2). The lessons are comprised of pages (level 3). If you go too deep into the hierarchy, the students can easily loose track of where they are in the course.

Title Placement

When you are several levels deep in a course, it is nice to have a reminder of where you are. This helps the students put the information they are seeing into context with all the information in the course. One way to assist with this is to display the course,

Outlook Shortcuts

Setting Up Outlook > Contacts

Adding a New Contact

In addition to using the New con
a contact, you can also use a
shortcut. If you receive an e-

module, and/or lesson name at all times. This takes up precious real estate, but can be designed to be unobtrusive.

Page Counters

Page counters (page 3 of 10, for example) provide a useful courtesy to your students. As they begin a course, module, lesson, etc., they will have a good idea as to how long they need to be able to commit to the course. Once they are in the course, they will be able to gauge their progress.

Bookmarking and Progress Indicators

Bookmarks allow the students to come back to the point where they last left off. Bookmarks can either be automatically set by the course when the Exit button has been selected, or they can be set manually by the student. For greatest flexibility, you can give the student the option to start from the beginning or to continue from the point of the bookmark.

Progress indicators generally appear on the course menu and indicate which sections have been started, completed, or passed by the student. In many cases, the bookmarking and progress markers are provided by the Learning Management System instead of by the course itself.

Special Features and Functions

Based on your audience, your objectives, and your programming options, you may want to include some or all of the following course features:

- Glossary
- Help
- How to use this course
- FAQs
- Reference documents
- Job aids
- Index
- Searchable text
- Handouts
- Note-taking screens

One of the best ways to decide what you want to include in your course is to review as many free online samples as you can find. But remember that just because you *can* do something doesn't mean you *should*. Keep your objectives and your audience in the front of your mind at all times. Make sure the technology supports the learning and doesn't overpower it.

The Design Document

By now you've made a lot of decisions about how your courses should be designed and developed. These decisions then need to be documented and agreed upon. This information will generally take the form of a design document.

The design document may also include the objectives and instructional strategies that were done during the first part of the design phase (Chapter 6). You may also choose to separate out some of the writing and graphic design issues into a style guide. The names and numbers of the documents don't really matter – what matters is that you make purposeful decisions and document them so everyone can work together.

The design document will be used by writers, instructional designers, editors, proofreaders, artists, and programmers. You may also use the design document to help you select an authoring tool or to help you write an RFP for a custom content development vendor.

Much of what is included in the design document will be related to the instructional design of the course. This information is in chapters 6 and 7 of this book. Other elements, such as the standards and storyboard information will be more production related. The storyboarding process is explained in chapter 8.

Refer to the sample outline in Figure 7.3 for some suggestions on what to include in your design document.

Figure 7.3 Sample Design Document Outline

Background

Briefly describe the overall training project, including the business need.

Rationale for WBT

Explain why WBT is being used as a training element. Include whether it will be used for initial training, refresher training, performance support, etc.

WBT Environment

Business Description
Describe the business in terms of number of locations, number of employees and culture.

Learning Environment
Describe the types of learning that has been used and their success in the past.

Audience Description

Describe audience members in terms of position, experience on the job, experience using computers, age, turnover, and any other factors relevant to the training.

Technology Description

Describe the systems used for hosting and viewing the courseware, including restrictions.

Content Structure

Course Objectives

Give a list of objectives with information about where they should go in the course.

Course Taxonomy
Describe how the course will be broken up: modules, units, etc.

Module Structure and Screen Sequence
Describe the standard introductory, content, and closing screens as they should be used for the whole course and for individual modules.

Seq. No.	Screen Type	Description
Screens for the Course as a Whole		
1.	Welcome screen for course	Visually interesting with minimum text.
2.	Course Overview *(may be more than one screen)*	Gets the student interested in the course. Explains high level concept of training and terminal objectives.
3.	How to Use This Course *(may be more than one screen)*	Instructs student how to operate and navigate the course.
Screens for Each Individual Module		
1.	Overview of Module	Gets the student excited about learning that procedure. Lists enabling objectives.
2.	Instructional/procedural frames	Provides training content.
3.	Summary or end of topic frame	Congratulates the learner. Reinforces most important points. Introduces and branches to the guided practice.
6.	Practice Overview	Provides instructions for the solo practice. Lists a refresher of the steps.
7.	Practice Steps	Provides sample data and gives feedback for each step. Last feedback branches to re-start the practice.

Instructional Strategies

<u>Presentation Materials</u>

Describe what types of instructional materials will be used in the course. For example, video, audio, text narration, diagrams, etc.

<u>Practice & Assessment</u>

Describe how the content will be practiced and how you will assess the student's learning.

Compliance Considerations

Describe if the course will need to be SCORM, AICC, or Section 508 compliant.

Testing and Assessments

<u>Question Types</u>

Describe the types of questions that should be used in the course, such as multiple choice, matching, etc.

<u>Placement</u>

Explain if you will be using pre-tests, post-tests, and/or individual questions embedded throughout the content.

<u>Remediation</u>

Describe the type of remediation you will be using throughout the course.

<u>Randomization</u>

Explain any randomization options you plan to use, including the order of options, order of questions, or the use of a test bank.

Interactions

<u>Interaction Types</u>

Describe the type of interactions, such as offline activities, that can be used in the course.

Media

Graphics and Animations

Describe such things as the overall graphics style, limits of file size, file format, etc.

Audio

If audio will be used, explain how it will be built into the course (for example, if it will be optional).

Video

If video will be part of the course, explain how it will be used.

Interface and Navigation

Graphics Design

Describe such things as what fonts and colors will be used, the page layout, and what buttons will look like.

Navigation Options

Explain how the student will access the courses and move around between different sections. Designate the use of "fixed" vs. "flexible" navigation.

Progress and Location Indicators

Describe what the student will see as they use the course. Describe menu options, title placement, page counters, and bookmarking.

Special Features and Functions

Explain any special features for the course, such as glossary, help, or FAQs.

Storyboards

Format

Explain what format will be used for the storyboards (Word/PowerPoint/etc.).

Naming conventions

Explain how the module documents should be named (both the storyboard document and the course files). Describe how the storyboards should be numbered (increments of 5, etc.).

Styles

If styles will be used in the storyboards, designate what styles should be used for each part of the storyboard. For example, you may want all screen titles to be formatted with "Heading 1" style and all paragraph headings with "Heading 2" style, etc.

Character restrictions

If there are limits to the number of words, lines, or characters for any individual element in the course, specify that here. For example, you may be able to fit 15 lines of text using a 2-inch column, or you may have a limit for 40 characters for a module title.

Writing Standards and Conventions

Terminology

Outline any special terminology requirements for the project. For example, do you want to use the phrase "Click Next" or "Click Forward"? Do you have a preference about computer terminology? Should employees be called Associates? Employees? Etc.

Writing Style

Describe the tone, style, and targeted education level for the writing.

Grammar and Formatting Standards

Designate what style guide or grammar reference will be used (*Gregg Reference Manual*, *Chicago Manual of Style*, *Microsoft Manual of Style for Technical Publications*, etc.). You may instead choose to spell out the specific grammatical and formatting standards you want to use in the course, or anything you want to do that is contrary to the style guide you have chosen.

Interactions

Describe how each interaction type should be worded any restrictions for each type (such as the number of words possible for a multiple choice answer).

Assessments

Describe how tests should be worded or formatted.

Additional Sections

Provide additional sections for any other part of the course that should have set content, language, or formatting, such as captions, headings, opening and closing screens, objectives, instructions, feedback, etc.

Development Process

<u>Project Management</u>
Describe how the project will be tracked.

<u>Interface and Prototype Development</u>
Describe how the interface and prototype will be developed, what content will be used, and what, if anything, can be done before it is finalized.

<u>Storyboard Development</u>
Include relevant information about source materials, subject-matter experts, and philosophy to be used for the storyboard development.

<u>Storyboard Review</u>
Outline who will be reviewing the storyboards at which phases of development and what they will be looking for. (And what might be considered an out-of-scope change.)

<u>Graphics Development & Review</u>
Describe technical, artistic, and instructional design issues for the use of graphics.

<u>Online Draft Development & Review</u>
Provide a checklist of what should be considered during the online review and what will be considered out-of-scope.

<u>Systems Integration</u>
Explain the steps to be taken to ensure the course works properly on the target systems.

Summary

The more you can plan and prepare before you begin your development, the more effective your course will be and the more efficient your production effort will become. Document decisions along the way and remember to always stay true to your audience and objectives and ensure that the technology supports the learning and doesn't detract from it.

8

The Development Phase: Writing the Course

Once you have designed your course, how are you going to breathe life into your ideas? How will you capture what elements you want in each particular course and how it will function? It is easy to be overwhelmed with the technical possibilities for the course.

Whether you are working with a programmer who will put your ideas into action or you are using rapid development strategies where one person takes care of everything, you will need to organize and write your content. This chapter will walk you through the process of getting your information and ideas in writing so you can make technology meet the objectives of your course.

Working with Storyboards

Storyboards allow you to express your ideas and let others know how to program your course to meet the learning goals. You can use them to provide learning points and direct programmers, artists, and other team members on how to build the course to your specifications. It is also helpful during the review process.

What Is a Storyboard?

In the 1920's, Walt Disney Studios started using storyboards with drawings for the scenes of the early Steamboat Willie cartoons. Major movie makers still use them today as an aid in creating the vision of the storylines in modern films. The storyboard system has grown and is now used in business for such things as project planning, manufacturing process design, and training course development.

In the world of e-learning, a storyboard is the blueprint of your course. It uses pictures, phrases, words, or sketches to communicate what you want your course to look like. After the objectives have been developed and the instructional strategies are in place, the storyboard can be developed. The storyboard:

- Contains your course content – The text that will be on each screen, including the interaction, question, or graphic that should be included.

- Provides directions to the programmers/artists – Programmers and artists need to know exactly what the developer wants the course to look like and how it should function. The storyboard does this. For example, the programmer will need to know where the **NEXT** button should take the learner so the path can be programmed properly.

- Creates the "vision" for the course – The design document outlined high-level instructional strategies and course features. In the storyboard, these strategies and features come to life. The developers can translate their visions into the information and instructions that will become the actual course.

- Reduces re-work – Every course goes through review and revision cycles (even just in the mind of the developer!). If the first review was done on a fully authored version of the course, you'd have a lot of expensive and time-consuming changes to make. If the reviews are done on the storyboards, the changes can be made before the media and programming work get started.

Figure 8.1 Sample Storyboard Template

Go to the Resources page at **www.e-LearningUncovered.com** for a downloadable version of this template.

[Course Name > Module # > Title]

[Board number]

Title:

Heading:

On-Screen Text:
Enter appropriate text here to introduce your module.

At the end of this module, you will be able to:

* Objective number one.
* Objective number two.
* Objective number three, etc.

This procedure will take approximately X minutes to learn. Click **FORWARD** to begin.

Visual: Standard objectives graphic (sample graphic shown)

Programming:
FORWARD: Goes to page ##.
SHOW ME: Inactive

The storyboard can be used to script your course content word-for-word or it can be used as a high-level course map. The template in Figure 8.1 shows a storyboard for specific content. Figure 8.2 shows an example of a high-level storyboard for a branching scenario.

Figure 8.2 Sample High-Level Storyboard

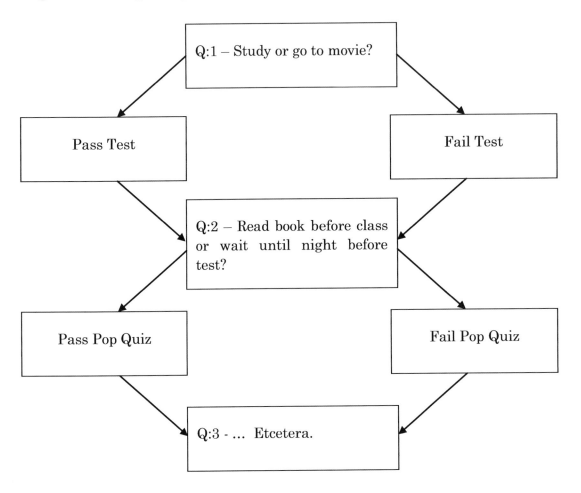

Elements of Storyboards

There isn't one specific way a storyboard should look. A storyboard could be a drawing (similar to a comic strip) or can include only text. It can be written on a piece of paper or can be done in templates on the computer that look much like the interface that will be used for the course. There are, however, certain things that should be included in a good storyboard.

Page Numbers

When you are working with storyboards, it is important that you and any of your programmers are able to follow the blueprint of your course. In addition, you'll need to keep track of many individual files that make up each course and screen (graphics, page files, etc.). To guarantee that everyone knows what to do and where to find the different elements, it is best to come up with standards about how to name and number everything from pages to graphics to audio files. Here are some tips to help you when designating page numbers:

- Number your storyboard pages in increments of 5 or 10 – For example, don't use screen number 1, 2, and 3. Instead, use screen numbers 5, 10, and 15 or 10, 20, and 30. This allows you to add or delete screens during the review process without making you renumber all of your screens and files. (Realize that these are not the page numbers that the student sees. These will be the file names for each page.)

- If you have different types of screens or screen layouts, you may want to include that in your numbering conventions – For example, if at the end of each section you have decided to include test questions, your test question page numbers may all be in the 200s. That way, any time you see a number that is in the 200 range you and your team members will automatically know test questions are included. This is also helpful if you need to quickly and easily pull out all of the test question storyboards for editing purposes.

- You may want to begin your page number with something that represents the project, course, or module you are working on – For example, if you are writing a training course on how to use Microsoft **Word**, you may want to start the page number with MSW. If it is the second module in the course, then the page number might be MSW-B-05. This is helpful for organization if you are working on multiple courses.

- Avoid using spaces in any file names – Some web-based programs do not handle spaces well. Instead, use a hyphen (-) or underscore (_) if you need to separate words.

On-Screen Text

The text of your course should include the learning points for the users as well as any instructions they need to know about. The text can be the easiest part of the storyboard to write – or the most difficult. This depends greatly on the complexity of the course, the types of interactions you are developing, and your natural writing style.

Text in your storyboard should include:

- Learning Points – The text of your storyboard should include information that supports your learning objectives.

- Learner Instructions – These instructions tell the learner how to move from screen to screen in the course. For example, if you have a NEXT button in the interface, you will want to tell the user to "click **NEXT** to continue" after they have read the page. Or, if you have included an interaction or question, you will want to explain how to use it.

- Alt-Text – If you have ever put your mouse over a graphic on a website and saw a small pop-up box that describes the graphic, that's alt-text. Alt-text is useful for anyone using screen reader technology due to visual impairments. If you want to attach alt-text to your graphics, include that text in your storyboard.

The text is not limited to the static text fields. Interactions can also include text. Rollovers are great ways to add learning text. For example, if you are developing a computer course, you may want to create rollovers that highlight the main parts of a window in the application. Each hotspot or rollover could include valuable text about that part of the application.

Media Elements

Each storyboard will need to include information about the graphics, audio, video, simulation, or other media files to be included. If the media element already exists, you can simply tell the programmer the name of the file to use. However, you can also use the storyboard to provide instructions or guidance if a media element needs to be found or created from scratch.

Audio

If you are including audio in your course, you may need to provide special instructions. If each screen has audio that is an exact match to the text, then the audio instructions can be very brief. You would need to indicate:

- How to pronounce any words that might be unfamiliar to the person doing the voice work.

- How you want any acronyms or abbreviations to be read.

- How to handle any special screen types. For example, for a question screen, do you want the question read, along with all the options and the remediation? For a roll-over screen, do you want to tie audio to each of the pop-up options, or just the instructions?

If your audio will not be an exact match to the text throughout the course, then you would need to write a full audio script. This audio script is a key part of your storyboard and should be included for all review cycles.

Video

If you are creating custom video for your course, you will need to script what needs to be said, as well as what the learner should see. For this, it would be good to think about how Disney would use a storyboard. You may need to sketch your ideas and will need to give detailed instructions about actions and scenes so the producer can understand what you want from your video clip. The more time you put into the storyboard for the video footage, the less time-consuming (and therefore less expensive) the video shoot and editing process will be.

Graphics

If you will be using existing graphics such as clip-art and stock photography collections or graphics available in the public domain, you will want to describe in your storyboards what the artist, researcher, or programmer should look for. For example:

> *A photo of a man in business casual clothing talking on the phone with an agitated look on his face.*

If a custom graphic is needed you will want to explain the graphic in detail and possibly provide a sketch.

Other Media Elements

Based on the design of your course, you may need to provide other instructions unique to the features you will be including. For example, if you will be using software simulations, then you will need to include the directions for what the simulation should do.

File Types and Naming Conventions

You may want to include details about the sizes and types of files to be used in the course. This can often be done in the design document if it is universal for the whole course. If it is likely to vary from screen to screen, then it should be included in the storyboard. For example, you may want to specify whether a graphic should be in .jpg or .gif format – and maybe even specify the pixel size of the graphic. You also have the option of leaving that up to the artist or programmer.

For media elements being custom created, you may want to provide guidance about how they should be named. Decide if you want media elements to match the screen numbers or have unique names. For example, if you create a computer simulation for Outlook to put on screen 225, you could agree to name it "OL-225-demo". This will help you know which screen it belongs to. However, if you are likely to re-use these elements, you may want a naming convention that is more universal, such as OL_add_a_contact_demo.

Programming Instructions

The programming instructions show a programmer how to take the learner from screen to screen during the course and even how each individual screen operates. Programmers follow the instructions you give to make sure the screen order and navigation is the way you design it. Detailed instructions could be needed, or you may just need to stipulate what template to use, or only put in instructions if you need to deviate from the norm (for example, if the next button does NOT go the next screen).

For this discussion, the programmer is the person assembling the course. If you are using a rapid-development tool, that person may not actually need to be a programmer in the traditional sense of the word.

Navigation

Let the programmer know the sequence of the screens and where the interface buttons should take the end user. Include any special requirements for any of the buttons as well. For example:

> *Next button: goes to screen OL-205.*
>
> *– or –*
>
> *Next button: inactive until question is answered correctly, then goes to OL-205.*

Links, Documents, or Special Features

Include any special instructions about documents to be attached to a page, hyperlinks to be included, or any other special features based on the design of your course. For example, if your course has a glossary and there is a word on the page that is in the glossary, you may want to include a hyperlink. You would indicate this on the storyboard. For example:

> *At the end of the on-screen text, include a hyperlink to the company's ethics policy.*
>
> *Text for hyperlink: View our company's policy.*
>
> *Document to link: R:\Policies and Procedures\Ethics.doc*
>
> *Have document open up in a separate browser window.*

Interactions

When you are storyboarding interactions, it is important to be very precise in your explanation of what you want. Programmers will often be creating interactions from scratch and you will want to make sure you explain the interaction to the programmer, include the teaching text that will be put in the interaction, as well as the instructions that should be given to the student.

Questions

Instructions about questions include several elements:

- <u>Question type</u> – Is it multiple-choice, true/false, etc.?

- <u>The question and the options</u> – The actual on-screen text for the questions and whatever choices the student has to select from.

- <u>On-screen instructions</u> – The text that lets the student know how to operate the question. For example, if it is a matching question, are they supposed to click on the answers or drag an imaginary line?

- <u>Remediation</u> – The text that appears when the student gets the question right or wrong.

- <u>Programmer instructions</u> – Any special guidelines about how the question should be set up. For example, the number of attempts a student can have or if the question is tied to a specific objective in a randomized bank of questions.

Storyboard Templates

Storyboard templates are a great way to make sure all of the elements you need for your storyboard are included. Templates can be outline-based, form-based, or give a visual representation of your course. They ensure that the format for your screen types is consistent throughout your course. Some course designs may require custom templates, or you may be able to find templates that have already been created.

If your authoring tool does not come with storyboard templates, then you'll want to decide what tool to use for storyboarding. Some tools that are good for developing storyboards are **Word**, **PowerPoint**, and **Visio**.

It is helpful to create a template for each different screen type you intend to use. These types might include, but are not limited to layouts for the following screens:

- Introduction
- Objective
- Standard teaching screen
- Demonstration
- Roll-overs
- Hot spots
- Video clips
- Practice
- Each question type
- Summary

The examples below are a visual templates made in **PowerPoint** to look like the finished course. This approach is useful when you have inexperienced team members or subject-matter experts creating content. Visualizing the final product can often help these team members create the content.

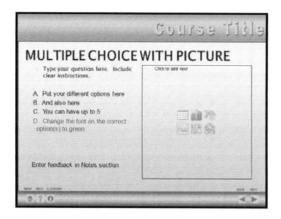 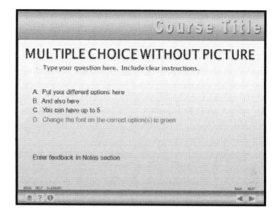

To decide what elements to include in your template, refer the Storyboard/Template Checklist in Figure 8.3.

Figure 8.3 Storyboard/Template Checklist

Go to the Resources page at **www.e-LearningUncovered.com** for a downloadable version of this checklist.

Instructions you might want to include	Include? Y/N
General	
File name for the screen/board	
Course title	
Module title	
Screen heading	
On-screen text	
Programming Instructions	
Links from other page(s)	
Links to next page(s)	
Active buttons	
Inactive buttons	
Pop-up windows	
Mouse-overs	
Hot-spots	
Audio	
Directions	
Script (text)	
File name	
File location	

Instructions you might want to include	Include? Y/N
Video	
Directions	
Script (text)	
File name	
File location	
Graphic/Media	
Description of graphic	
Graphic pasted directly into storyboard	
Sketch of graphic	
File name and location of existing graphic	
File name to be used for custom graphic	
Alt-text	
Captions	
Labels	
Interactions	
Description of interaction	
Text	
Interaction name/title	
File name and location of existing interaction	
File name to be used for custom interaction	
Questions	
Instructions	
Questions	-
Optional answers to questions	
Correct answers to questions	
Remediation	

Developing Your Content

Organizing Content

Now that you know everything that belongs in a storyboard, how do you gather and organize the information? Most English writing instructors tell students to outline their thoughts and ideas before they start writing. Here is how you outline information in storyboard fashion:

- <u>Develop your objectives</u> – This was done during the design phase (Chapter 6).

- <u>Create taxonomy and outline</u> – This was also done during the design phase (Chapter 6).

- <u>Write your test questions</u> – This, too, was done during the design phase (Chapter 7).

- <u>Write the main point on each storyboard</u> – Once you have outlined your course at a high level, you can divide your screens or pages by objective or main point. This may seem like an easy step to skip. But because of the time and effort needed to create each and every screen, it will be very important that your writing is clear, organized, and succinct. Sketching out the main point that goes on each screen will help you stay targeted and will help you keep development time and costs under control.

- <u>Add supporting points as desired</u> – This allows you to take the information to a deeper level in your outline.

- <u>Go back and write the actual text</u> – The information you have gathered from your topic research, subject matter experts, and various documentation can now be added to the storyboards.

- <u>Add the interactions and reinforcement questions</u> – The interactions you create should support the learning goal.

- <u>Add navigation instructions</u> – You will want to include the navigation instructions on each storyboard.

- <u>Write special feature pages</u> – You may have designed special feature buttons such as glossary, FAQ, job aids, etc. You will need to write storyboards for each of those buttons so they will contain the desired information.

Throughout the process you will want to make sure you are using good instructional design strategies. Think about your audience analysis when making decisions about the content of your storyboard. Many decisions about what is included in your storyboard would have been made during the design phase.

Chapter 8

Converting Existing Content

When you are converting existing content from instructor-led training (ILT) to e-learning, you will find a new set of challenges. It is normal to think that if you already have a course designed for the classroom that it could quickly and easily be converted to e-learning with little or no additional effort. Unfortunately, this is rarely the case. Here are some special concerns when converting existing content.

Course Length

Because of the cost of e-learning development, you'll want to make sure that you only include the elements that are truly necessary for the learning to take place. You don't want to strip out content to save time and money, but you will want to look at the entire program carefully and possibly eliminate some of the "nice-to-know" information.

Anticipating Questions

While you may be teaching a more scaled-down version of the course, you might need to be more thorough in your explanation of some areas. Students taking an e-learning course don't have the benefit of asking an instructor clarifying questions. Make sure you give important information and adequate explanations up-front so the student can meet learning goals. One way of making sure you answer the learners' questions up-front would be to ask the classroom instructors what questions they typically receive during a class session.

Including ALL the Content

Sometimes the most valuable information a learner gets from ILT comes from the instructor, rather than the written materials. For example, if a **PowerPoint** presentation is your only documentation, you may only have 40% of the content taught! Some of the best interest, color, and application for a teaching point can come from an off-the-cuff story told by an instructor. So if you are using the written materials alone to develop your e-learning course, you may be missing important information. You may want to interview instructors to see what personal stories or special information they are giving their classes that may not be included in the written materials.

Interactions

Any good classroom training includes interactions where the students have a chance to think, reflect, respond, and process. Some of those activities might work in an online environment, but some of them won't. You will need to decide how to make sure your online students get the same level of engagement, practice, and application as your classroom students.

Informal Changes to the ILT Materials

Over time, instructors learn what does and doesn't work in the classroom. They may have made a number of changes to content, format, or teaching strategies based on feedback they've received – as well as from their own judgment. These changes may not have ever been incorporated into the ILT materials, but may be something you want to look into prior to developing the e-learning class. Just because something is written in the ILT manuals, doesn't mean it was a successful element of the classroom learning experience.

If you have existing courseware, you should be able to develop your e-learning in less time, but realize that it will not be a straight conversion. You will need to put extra thought and perhaps extra research into the process.

Summary

Storyboarding provides the blueprint for your course. Make sure you include all of the necessary elements so your blueprint is complete. Whether you are having other people program your course or are using rapid development techniques, using storyboards helps you organize your content and make sure everyone is working toward the same goal.

Remember to follow these guidelines for storyboarding success:

- <u>Develop naming conventions</u> – Naming conventions identify each screen and graphic and make it easy to locate information quickly.

- <u>Make it interesting for the end users</u> – Remember to use good instructional design to make the program interesting for the learner.

- <u>Watch your character count</u> – Remember that there is limited space on a screen. Write in a journalistic style to get your information to the learner succinctly.

- <u>Graph the vision of your course</u> – Use the storyboard as a blueprint for others so they can program the course and follow your instructions accurately.

- <u>Use templates</u> – Templates will allow you to make sure you include everything you need for a screen, including programming instructions.

The Development Phase: Putting the Course Together

"WOW! All this work and you don't even have a course yet!?" Sometimes it may feel that way, but putting all the planning and design time in up front will help to ensure the success of your project. But now with everything laid out, it is time to start putting the course together!!

During the production process, you'll want to keep a close eye on everything to make sure it meets all the right criteria. This formative evaluation process includes everything from simple proofreading to content reviews to technical testing to usability studies.

You'll likely start off with a small manageable prototype and then revise and expand your guidelines as you prepare for full-scale production.

Rapid Prototyping

If you have a lot of courseware to develop and not a lot of time to do it, you may be tempted to jump right in and get everyone started. But if you are working on a course for the first time, or are working on a course with significant design changes over previous courses, you might do well to start with a prototype.

A prototype is a sample "chunk" of courseware that is developed from start to finish before the rest of the courseware is begun. Rapid prototyping means developing a rather small, but representative chunk of content – perhaps 15 minutes worth.

Why Create a Prototype?

During the design phase, you made a lot of assumptions and decisions. The prototype helps you to make sure that those assumptions are valid and that the decisions translate well when they move from the drawing board into actual production. Developing a prototype from beginning to end before beginning work on the rest of the courseware has several benefits:

- <u>Save re-work</u> – During the prototype phase, you will probably find elements that don't work as intended or guidance that wasn't clear to writers, artists, or programmers. If you have already begun production on a number of lessons or modules, all of them will have to be revised once you learn of the issues. If you work with a prototype, you can catch the issues early and revise your design or processes before the rest of the work begins.

- <u>Help streamline processes</u> – During the development of the prototype, you will probably uncover various shortcuts that help the entire team work together. You may find that it is easier for your programmer to build the course if the storyboards use a certain style. Or you may learn from the person in charge of audio recording that if the script is provided in double-spaced format, there are fewer errors made during recording.

- <u>Help with development estimates</u> – By taking one chunk of content from beginning to end, you can test your development timelines and make revisions to the estimates. Realize, however, that the first part of any new course tends to take the longest.

- <u>Can be tested</u> – If it turns out your courseware is too complicated for your target audience, or the design style is too frivolous for the culture, then the prototype phase is the best place to find this out. Similarly, you can find out at this point if the course works technically in the target environment. This is accomplished with user testing and integration testing; both are covered in more detail later in this chapter. The sooner in the project you uncover an issue, the easier it is to resolve. If you wait until you are ready to launch a program, then you will have expensive, time-consuming revisions on your hands.

- <u>Help you feel the progress</u> – It can be good for team morale and customer comfort to see some very real, tangible progress on an e-learning project. The prototype is something you can show to everyone to build excitement, support, and momentum.

There is one major disadvantage to working with a prototype – time. Putting together a prototype can often take 6 to 8 weeks because of all the decisions that have to be made and all the processes that need to be worked out. This may feel like a very long time before you can really start the development. However, on most projects, it is worth the investment up front to save time, money, and headaches for the rest of the project.

Selecting the Content for a Prototype

When deciding what content to use for the prototype, think "typical." You don't want to select the simplest material, and you don't want to select the most complex material. Instead, select something that is typical of the course in general and that incorporates the major features and functions of the course. For example, you probably don't want to select the beginning of the course since that material is often very general and may not lend itself to the interactions, practices, and quizzes you have planned for the rest of the course.

Rapid Development

The process of developing an e-learning course from concept to execution can be a time-consuming endeavor. So if there is a need for immediate training, what can be done to minimize the gap between the time the course is needed and the time the course can comfortably be created? Is there a way to speed up the process?

Rapid development is the answer. It allows an e-learning course to be developed faster, and sometimes cheaper, without sacrificing quality. Here are some things that can decrease development time:

- Developing several courses or modules at the same time – Ideally, you would want to develop one course all the way to completion to serve as a prototype, and then begin the additional modules. If you need to save time, you may have your team start working on the storyboards for additional modules before you finish the prototype. If you use this strategy, plan on some re-work being done on the storyboards based on lessons learned from the prototype – but at least you'll have a good start on your other modules' content.

- Choosing an easy-to-**learn** course authoring tool – If you have a tool that is easy to learn, you'll be up and running quickly, and you can probably find more people in your organization that can help you. Even the subject matter experts themselves can pitch in if it is easy enough to learn.

- Choosing an easy-to-**use** course authoring tool – Whether or not something is easy to learn is a one-time issue. Be sure also to consider how easy it is to *use* once you are up and running. The same module might take 1 hour in one software or 3 hours in another software.

- Using ready-made templates – When you use templates that are already created, you can just plug information into the template, rather than having to make individual interface design decisions. With the templates, the design has already been produced.

- Wearing lots of hats – If you have someone on your development team that can design, develop, and program your e-learning course, let her do it! If the same person is writing the storyboards, working with the media elements, and assembling the course, you can save time for two reasons. First of all, the storyboard instructions don't have to be as detailed if one person is doing all the work. Secondly, any time work has to pass from one person to another, you lose a little time and increase the project coordination effort.

- <u>Working on media and authoring before the review cycle is complete</u> – Ideally, you would have your storyboards reviewed internally as well as by your client, and SMEs before you begin the process of finding or creating the graphics and actually assembling the course. However, the storyboard review cycles can take a lot of time and are prone to delays. If you need to accelerate your project, you can use the drafts of the storyboards to begin the work on the media and authoring. This will give you a head start on that work, but realize you may need to re-do some of it based on changes requested by the client or the subject matter expert.

- <u>Keeping on top of deadlines</u> – The shorter the time allotted for course completion, the more crucial it is for you to make sure no deadlines are missed. Even one deadline being missed can be a problem when you are working toward rapid development.

The course authoring tool you choose is the most critical factor when you are working toward a rapid development goal. Look for one that contains good templates (or allows you to make your own) and is easy to develop.

"Paper" Review Cycles

While you are still at the storyboard phase of development, changes are still relatively easy to fix. Therefore, it is usually a good idea to conduct a series of thorough reviews before the course is actually built. Once media has been developed and the course has been assembled, changes become more involved. However, if you need a very quick turnaround, you can choose to hold off on all reviews until the course is built.

In most cases, you will want to review storyboards for:
- Content
- Instructional Design
- Editorial Accuracy

Structuring Your Reviews

You'll want a clearly-defined process for how reviews should be handled. This process can be defined and documented during the design phase. There are many ways to structure your review cycles and many factors for you to consider, such as:

- How many people should look at a given module?

- When do we want to involve external reviewers (business customers and subject-matter experts)? Do we want to review it internally first? Do we want to involve them at storyboard phase or once the course is developed?

- What do we do if people disagree with each other in their comments?

- How long do we allow for reviewers to go over the material?

- What do we do if they don't respond in the time allotted?

- How do we want feedback to be provided? (Hand-written notes, Excel spreadsheet, tracked changes in Word, etc.)

- How will we keep track of open issues and questions?

- What do we do if we think a suggested change isn't a good idea?

- How will you handle extensive changes? (Will it impact the project schedule? Should it be considered out-of-scope? Would it warrant any additional charges, if appropriate?)

- What process will we have for checking that the corrections were made correctly?

- Do we need formal sign-off on the final version?

- Do we want to start on any media or programming work before final sign-off?

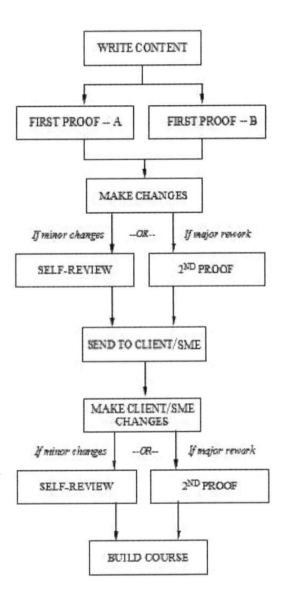

Figure 9.1 Sample Storyboard Review Process

Content Review

You can have the flashiest graphics and the coolest interactions in the world, but if your content is bad your course will be a flop. That's why one of the early steps in the review process is to have your content checked for accuracy. Even if you are converting material from an existing document, you will still want a thorough review – a simple edit could inadvertently change the meaning of something.

You'll want to provide clear instructions to your reviewers so they know what to look for. Some reviewers might get caught up in grammar or typographical issues instead of focusing on the content itself. You can increase the chances of getting the kind of feedback you want if your provide elements you want reviewers to focus on.

Figure 9.2 Content Review Questions

- Are the objectives valid?
- Are the objectives complete? If someone masters all the stated objectives, will they have all the information they need to know?
- Is all of the information accurate, thorough, and current?
- Are there any terms or concepts used that the target audience may not already understand?
- Is there anything critical to mastering the objectives that has not been covered?
- Is there any information included in the course that the target audience doesn't really need to know?
- Are the explanations of the content clear and accurate?
- Are the diagrams, captions, and graphics accurate?
- Are all industry-specific terms spelled properly?
- If there is audio, are all industry-specific terms pronounced properly?
- Do the activities reinforce the most critical information?
- Do the questions test the most critical information?
- Would someone be prepared to do his or her job after completing this course?
- Have we left anything out?

Instructional Design Review

Just because you have thorough, accurate content doesn't mean it is taught well! This is why you'll want your courses to be reviewed for instructional design. If you are a one-person team, then this will need to be a self-check. Ideally, you would have a separate team member with knowledge of instructional design to review the work.

Figure 9.3 Instructional Design Review Checklist

- Review all questions from the Content Review Checklist.
- Will the students understand what is expected of them?
- Are the objectives well-written and clearly stated?
- Are the benefits of learning this information clearly explained?
- Does the teaching content support the objectives?
- Will the students know how to apply the information to their particular situation?
- Are the students given opportunities to practice the concepts?
- Do the students receive adequate feedback on their practice sessions?
- Are the questions too easy or too hard?
- Are any of the questions too subjective?

Editorial Review

In addition to the content and the instructional design, you will want to make sure your information is written, structured, and formatted correctly. This job can be filled by anyone with strong written language skills who has a copy of all your standards documentation.

The editorial review and the instructional design review can be done by the same person, but preferably not at the same time. It's hard to wear both hats at once, so you will get more thorough feedback if the reviewer goes through the material once for instructional design and then a second time for editorial issues.

Some teams prefer to save the editorial review until last, getting the big issues out of the way before starting on the smaller issues. That way you don't have to worry about grammar or word choice on a screen that is going to be re-written by the subject-matter experts anyway.

On the other hand, you may want to do an editorial review before sending storyboards to a client or subject-matter expert so you don't have to worry about being "embarrassed" by spelling and grammar problems.

Figure 9.4 Editorial Review Questions

- Are there any spelling or typographical errors?

- Does the writing use good grammar and word choice?

- Could the same thing be said more simply?

- Is the material written to the intended reading level?

- Are there any phrases or idioms that a non-native speaker of English might not understand?

- Is the formatting consistent with the standards documentation and any designated style guide?

- For any formatting not specifically designated in the documentation, is it used consistently throughout the course?

Assembling the Course

The methods and processes you would use for assembling the course will vary greatly based on what kind of authoring tool you are using, as well as the specific course features and functions you are incorporating. At this stage in the project, you will be creating your media elements based on direction from the storyboards, and actually assembling all the content into whatever course building system you are using.

You will be guided by all the decisions you made up until this point, specifically those found in your project plan, design document, and storyboards. Now it comes time to simply follow the directions! However, there are a few special concerns you might want to think about as well.

Course Extras

During production, it is easy to focus mainly on the individual modules or lessons. However, the development phase also includes any course "extras" that are a part of the design. Work them into your plan up front so you don't forget about them until it is time to launch your courses!

Based on your design plan, you may need to develop:

- <u>Title page</u> – if you want a graphic or animated first impression for the course.
- <u>Catalog description</u> – to help the students decide if a course is appropriate for them.
- <u>Fine print</u> –to provide any legal statements such as copyright, confidentiality statement, privacy policy (especially if you will be tracking scores and answers), disclaimers, acknowledgements for other copyrighted material used with permission, statements about trademarks referred to, etc.
- <u>How to use this course</u> – to provide details on the various features and functions of the course, how to move around, etc.
- <u>Help section</u> –to provide troubleshooting on issues that might arise with the course.
- <u>FAQs (Frequently Asked Questions)</u> – to give information either about how the course operates or about the content itself.
- <u>Glossary and/or index</u>.
- <u>References and job aids</u>.
- <u>Any other feature you might be including</u>.

File Names and Version Control

Once production begins, you will be creating a lot of files: storyboard files, media elements, course files, output files. And when you begin the review cycles, you are likely to have several versions of each. Special care will need to be taken to make sure that you know where to find everything and which version is the most current.

If you are using a Learning Content Management System, you can manage files, versions, and reviews in the system itself. Otherwise, you will need to create standards and conventions to help. Here are a few suggestions.

- <u>Use separate folders to indicate where a given file is in the process</u> – For example, you can have a "Storyboards" folder with sub-folders called "SB-rough draft," "SB–1st proof," "SB–ready for client" and "SB–final ready to program."

- <u>Use the file name to show where it is in the process</u> – For example, each reviewer can add his or her initials to the file name when finished reviewing it. "UnitA-de" could mean that it has been reviewed once and "UnitA-de-dw" could mean that is has been reviewed twice.

- <u>Keep a spreadsheet to track your progress and include a place to include file names and locations</u> – This will help you quickly locate the exact information you need later.

On-Screen Review Cycles

Content Reviews

Even though your content was probably reviewed very thoroughly during the storyboard phase, you will want to have it reviewed again once it is on-screen. Because of the storyboard "paper" reviews, this cycle should go rather quickly, but you still want to re-visit the three main review areas: content, instructional design, and editorial issues. First of all, you want to make sure that everything from the storyboards was translated properly into the working on-screen version. Secondly, you'll want to make sure that the ideas and concepts planned out in the storyboard are actually effective.

A new part of the content review at this point is a review of the media elements. You'll want to take a thorough look at graphics, interactions, audio, and video as you go through the three main review areas. Check for everything from typos in the graphics to proper pronunciation in the audio to changes needed to the instructions on an interaction because it was programmed differently than originally planned.

Functionality Review

In addition to your content review, you'll want to make sure the course has been programmed properly and functions as expected. The best Quality Assurance tester is one who enjoys trying to "break" the system, gets the course to do something it shouldn't do, and looks at everything a student might possibly misunderstand or do wrong.

The types of issues you should look for will vary based on the specific features and functions of your course, your development process, your authoring tool, and lessons learned from previous mistakes. For example, if your course authoring process includes an automatic screen counter, you may not need to go through the whole course and make sure it is accurate on each page (except perhaps for the prototype where you test to make sure the function is working). However, if you have to manually enter the page counter, then you would want to check it on every screen.

To help manage the review and revision process, create a checklist for the reviewers and a tracking log for requesting, making, and confirming corrections. A sample format is provided for your reference. You will need to add your own elements based on your unique situation. For example, Figure 9.6 includes a column for issue type. If you are working with a large development team with clearly defined roles, this is a useful column so that team members can find the issues that relate to them: audio, graphics, text, programming, etc. If you are a one or two person team where everyone does everything, then this column is not really necessary.

Figure 9.5 Sample On-Screen Review Process

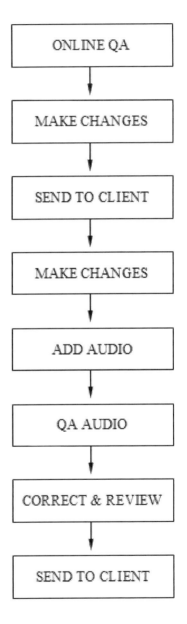

ONLINE QA

MAKE CHANGES

SEND TO CLIENT

MAKE CHANGES

ADD AUDIO

QA AUDIO

CORRECT & REVIEW

SEND TO CLIENT

Figure 9.6 On-Screen QA Issues List

Go to the Resources page at **www.e-LearningUncovered.com** for a downloadable version of this issues list.

	Logged By	Screen #	Issue Type	Issue	Resolved Y/N	Comments
2	DW	1-12	Onscreen	The link isn't work working in the first pop-up.	Y	
3	DW	1-12	Video	The video isn't playing when I click the icon.	N	The video is the wrong file type. Updated file requested from the producer.
4	DW	1-14	Onscreen	The fonts are not consistent on the page.	Y	
5	DW	1-14	Navigation	The next button is going to the final exam rather than to chapter 2.	Y	

Plan on how you would like to handle a review of the reviews. It is dangerous to assume that all problems got fixed properly without creating any new problems. It is more time consuming but generally worthwhile to have someone confirm EVERY correction, including every correction to a correction.

Figure 9.7 On-Screen Functionality Checklist

Go to the Resources page at **www.e-LearningUncovered.com** for a downloadable version of this checklist.

ISSUE TYPE	ISSUE	MODULE								
		A	B	C	D	E	F	G	H	I
	Overall Module									
Navigation	Each section launches from menu									
Navigation	All screens are present									
Navigation	Screen counter is accurate									
Navigation	Forward through the course									
Navigation	Back through the course									
Navigation	Module title is accurate									
	Per screen (all screen types)									
Programming	Slide heading correct									
Programming	Text taken from the correct storyboard									
Programming	No text cut off									
Text formatting	Text formatted properly (bullets, bolding)									
Text	Text clear, true, and error free									
Media	Correct media shown									
Buttons	Unneeded buttons are inactive									

ISSUE TYPE	ISSUE	MODULE								
		A	B	C	D	E	F	G	H	I
	Rollover/pop-up screens									
Rollover	Rollover text matches image									
Rollover	Text does not overlap									
Rollover	Clear what has been accessed or not									
Text	Easy to understand what to do									
Buttons	Forward button does not work until complete									
	Computer simulation screens									
Buttons	Show Me button launches simulation									
Media	Simulation plays to the end									
Buttons	Pause works									
Buttons	Replay works									
Buttons	Forward button does not work until complete									
	Practice screens									
Programming	Get all answers right									
Programming	Get all answers wrong									
Programming	First incorrect feedback									
Programming	Second incorrect feedback									
Programming	Try to do something you shouldn't be able to									
Buttons	Show Me button inactive									
Buttons	Forward button does not work until complete									

Technical Testing

While the course may work properly for the designers, developers, and testers, you'll also want to make sure it functions properly on the target platform. Generally, this testing will be conducted or at least coordinated with your I.T. Department. Areas to be tested include:

- Integration testing – Does it operate properly with any other related systems (such as a Learning Management System)?

- Load testing – Will the courses, when used by the projected number of people, cause the systems to slow down or even crash? Can the servers handle it? Can the company bandwidth handle it?

- Workstation testing – Will the courses run on the various configurations of workstations? You'll want to test the courses on the various configurations possible, such as different browser versions, operating systems, or bandwidth. If you are dealing with students learning from their home computers, be sure to test for all the variations that might exist on a home computer. If students will be dialing in through a network (such as Citrix), consider any restrictions or special configurations for that network.

Technical testing is an area where your prototype will be extremely valuable. It is quite possible that you'll find issues that affect some significant aspect of your design. Make sure you get that feedback EARLY in the development process.

End-User Testing

If you conduct testing with subject-matter experts, instructional designers, editors, and technical testers, you will greatly improve the quality of the course. But despite all of that hard work, that doesn't mean the final students will like it, enjoy it, be able to use it, or get what they need from it! That's why one of the most critical elements of your test plan is end-user testing.

User testing will help you determine whether:

- They like or enjoy the course.
- They understand the material.
- The material is helpful to them.
- They can operate the course.

According to Saul Carliner, author of <u>Designing e-Learning</u>, "A study compared the problems with a draft found by usability experts and those actually encountered by users. The 'best' expert could only find 48 percent of the roadblocks that users found. This means that only way to effectively identify roadblocks is through a usability test."

Planning Your User Testing

When to test

User testing is best done early in the process – preferably at the prototype stage. You'll want to run the course through all other testing first, so that your users won't get caught up on typos or obvious functionality issues.

Who to test

You'll want your test subjects to represent the full cross-section of your audience in terms of computer proficiency, age, cultural background, existing knowledge of the subject matter, role in the company, and any other variable that relates to your program.

Planning the logistics

Make sure that the students will have everything they need to complete the course. This includes a proper technical set-up (such as the proper plug-ins or speakers) as well as any supplemental materials required for the course (a printed manual, paper and pencil, etc.). You may also need to set up user names and passwords for each tester.

Check with your facilitator to coordinate the length of the test, the number of students that can be observed by a single facilitator, any supplies needed (such as forms and pencils).

Conducting Your User Testing

Whenever possible, you'll want someone that has not been involved with the development to conduct the testing. The users are likely to be more comfortable sharing feedback and the facilitators are more likely to remain neutral about the process and the feedback.

Additionally, it is best to work with someone who has experience with user testing and knows the best way to gather complete, accurate, detailed feedback. You can't expect your test subjects to just tell you everything you need to know by filling out a quick form. You'll want to work with a facilitator who is skilled at getting strong feedback.

Ideally, the facilitator will gather feedback by observing the students taking the course, by encouraging the students to make verbal comments about their thoughts while they are taking the course, and by conducting a final interview to get more details and clarify comments.

Acting on Your Results

Imagine you are reviewing the summary of the results and you see that about a third of the test subjects say the course was too slow. Another third say it was too fast. And another third say it was just right. It's enough to make you feel like Goldilocks and go take a nap!

Review and consider all comments, but then make your best judgment. You'll have comments that contradict each other. Some suggestions would be too expensive or time consuming to implement, some would result in a worse product, and some comments might even come across as rude or insensitive.

You'll have to strike a delicate balance between deciding that a comment is not valid or universal enough to warrant a change versus disregarding a comment because deep down you resent it.

Unfortunately, you will not always get clear feedback from your test subjects. Sometimes they will comment on what they think the solution is, rather than what the problem is. Sometimes they'll be too vague to really give you an idea of what could be different.

For example, if a student says the course is too long, is it really too long? Maybe it only felt long because it wasn't interesting and the student couldn't figure out how it applied to him or her. In this case, deciding to shorten the course wouldn't fix the *real* problem.

Try, whenever possible, to get more information from the test subject, or at least get more creative when reviewing a comment and try to make sure you are really getting to the heart of the issue.

Be sure to build time and money into your project plan for the re-work that will come from your testing; both at the prototype phase and during the testing for each individual module. It is nice to think that everything will work out as planned, but experience tends to prove otherwise.

Summary

It can be very exiting to see your vision finally taking shape and coming to life. By starting with a prototype, not only will you have the chance to build excitement by seeing some tangible results quickly, but you'll gain valuable insight about your design and development that will streamline your production and increase the effectiveness of your course.

In addition to the actual production work itself, take the time necessary to build in all the checks and balances needed to ensure you end up with a quality product that works properly, that people enjoy, and that meets the business goal.

Put formal processes in place to review your course for content, instructional design, editorial issues, proper functionality, technical problems, and end-user feedback.

10

The Implementation Phase

So, your courses are finished. You've put your time and energy into making everything perfect. You can finally breathe easy because your work is done and now you just get to sit back and relax and let everybody take your courses...or can you? Almost, but not quite!

You still want to make sure everything and everyone is ready for the courses. Do the students know why they are taking them and how to access them? Will they get the support from management they need to find the time for them? Not only that, but what will happen once a student completes a course?

Though implementation day is the day everything comes together and the courses are available for your first student, you will want to consider and execute some implementation items prior to the day your courses are ready.

Preparing the Audience

If you build it, they will come...or will they? You'll increase your chances if they know where to come, why it is important to them, and that they have the support of management to do so. You will want to market your course to the organization so people will get excited and know what to do.

Your preparation approach might be different based on where your course falls in the e-learning roll-out. If the course is the first e-learning course ever, you may want to take more time and care to prepare your audience than if e-learning is something your organization has already embraced as a regular training method.

Bosses

Getting buy-in from the management team is often the best way to get training disbursed through an organization. The management team (hopefully) wants what is best for the organization, for themselves, and for the people working for them. They have great influence over the audience members who may or may not be ready and able to participate in training.

Often the best way to get buy-in from management is to give business reasons for the training. For example, in a customer service organization, a particular course may likely lead to more satisfied customers, which could ultimately make their lives easier. Letting the managers know about this benefit could give them the incentive to encourage the learners.

Learners

Getting information to the learners about the course, the learning process, etc., can be challenging. You can market the course through e-mail, company literature, and an Internet or Intranet site. And don't forget to use your management team.

The management team can introduce the training and create urgency for course completion. Giving information on how learning the information in the course can help them, or how it will make their job easier might be good self-motivation. Or, making a course mandatory might be a step toward making sure a course is completed if it is that important to an organization.

Environment

Has e-learning been launched before in the organization? And, how do the learners feel about e-learning? How do they feel about training in general? The answers to these questions could define your learning environment.

The learning environment can make or break an e-learning project. If e-learning is new, you may want to take extra time marketing the concept and the process, as well as the course. Perhaps you can offer a classroom session for everyone to try out the first course. This helps bridge the gap between how they are used to learning and how they will soon be learning.

If e-learning has been rolled out and was unsuccessful in the past, you will want to fix what went wrong during the first roll-out, market the course as "new," and focus on course improvements and benefits. Consider taking a core group of influential employees (not necessarily managers, but peers that are well-respected) and having them serve as a pilot group. If they like the new training, they'll spread the word in a way that people will listen.

If your organization has rolled out e-learning successfully and the environment is positive, you may only need to mention a course exists and everybody will want to take it!

Incentives and Disincentives

Incentives are anything that encourages a learner to take a course or series of courses. An incentive could be something as simple as a certificate of completion or a type of bonus. Incentives can give e-learning a positive reputation in the company as they encourage participation and get people excited.

Disincentives, on the other hand, are anything that may make someone *not* want to take a course. Sometimes courses have unintentional, built-in disincentives. For example, if students need to spend an hour taking a course and yet they still have to achieve the same production levels as if they were on the manufacturing floor all day, that is a disincentive. If there are consequences to not getting their work done, but no consequences if you don't complete the training, that is a disincentive.

Take a look at everything from manager attitudes to performance criteria to bonus policies to see where you can add incentives and remove disincentives.

Hoo-Hah

What is hoo-hah? Some very technical e-learning terminology? No, it's just a catch-all word for anything fun and interesting you might want to do to get people excited. Especially if an e-learning initiative is a new concept, the hoo-hah is important so the course gets the attention it needs to be successful.

Hoo-hah might include creating a fun name for the overall initiative, with its own logo. Put up signs, posters, or balloons. You might have drawings or other contests for the first people to complete a course. You could have a kick-off party with the CEO or other high-profile executives (and lots of food!).

Take some time to think about the best way to include a little fanfare with your rollout. Every organization has a culture or personality and your culture will need to dictate how much and what type of hoo-hah is best.

---

10 Tips for Making Your Implementation a Success

1. *Develop an engaging e-learning course. (If the course is bad, no amount of marketing will lead to long-term success.)*

2. *Make your course match your audience's learning needs.*

3. *Market your e-learning course.*

4. *Provide support. (Your support needs will be greatest in the first few months but then will hopefully dwindle some.)*

5. *Give clear directions on how to access the course.*

6. *Give incentives for course completion.*

7. *Minimize disincentives.*

8. *Involve management to promote buy-in.*

9. *Support a positive environment for e-learning.*

10. *Prepare your technology for your course so your first students have a positive experience and spread the word.*

Ongoing Management

Once your course is up-and-running, you will want to continue to manage and update your course.

Troubleshooting

No matter how much time you spent reviewing and testing your course, there will probably be some type of technical problems. Perhaps it is a home user with a different browser or the realization that the courses won't run on your remote network. While you can't prevent these issues 100%, you can be prepared for them. Make sure you have sufficient project resources (time, manpower, and money) to troubleshoot issues as they arise.

Revisions and Updates

As a course ages, it may need to be revised or updated. Revisions could be done simply to make the course better based on feedback received or updates may be needed for information that has changed and is no longer valid. Sometimes the problem with this is that nobody plans on this happening, so it isn't being managed.

Have a plan in place to deal with changes such as policies changes, computer upgrades, or learner feedback. Decide in advance who will be the long-term "owner" of the training program. In some organizations, it is a different group than the one that created the courses initially.

Reporting

You can set your course up to give feeds to your LMS to track any number of things – but if you don't check what it is tracking, it doesn't help you evaluate your course. You may want to validate test questions to make sure they are good, check your pass/fail rate or completion rate, etc. Chapter 11 will give more information on the evaluations you might be reviewing and what you might look for.

Summary

Once your courses are complete, it takes more to implement them than just posting them on the servers. After making sure your course functions properly, your technology is set, and that your audience is informed and excited, you can then let your audience start learning!

Remember, however, that training development is never truly over. Put plans in place to troubleshoot issues, update content, and manage the administrative elements.

So, now you can finally breathe easy because your work is done. You just get to sit back and relax and let everybody take your course...until it's time for the next course!!

11

The Evaluation Phase

You did it! You have e-learning content up and running! So now the question becomes, is it everything you hoped for? And is it everything that everyone else hoped for?

You used a number of evaluation techniques to guide you during the development of the project (formative evaluation). Now it is time to evaluate the reaction, effectiveness, and impact of the final product (summative evaluation).

One of the most commonly used models for evaluating training is the Kirkpatrick model, developed by Donald Kirkpatrick.

Level 1: Reaction

Level 2: Learning

Level 3: Transfer

Level 4: Results

Many training practitioners work with an additional 5th level, as suggested by Return on Investment expert, Jack Phillips:

Level 5: Return on Investment

These forms of evaluation apply to any type of training: instructor-led or e-learning. This chapter will include some high-level guidelines about each level of evaluation plus specific information about what is unique to e-learning.

Level 1 Evaluation: Student Reaction

Level 1 evaluation is designed for you to receive feedback about what the students *thought* about the course.

Goal of Level 1 Evaluation

You will want to find the students' opinions on whether they liked it, whether they *thought* it was effective, whether they *thought* they would use the information, etc. A level 1 evaluation is, by nature, very subjective – measuring opinions and impressions.

A positive reaction from the students can definitely impact whether or not they learn (level 2) as well as whether or not they are willing and eager to move forward with other, similar courses.

As with the results of your pilot testing (Chapter 9), you'll gather some information that is helpful, some that is vague, and some that is downright confusing.

Specific Questions to Ask

Questions for Evaluating any Training Format

Likert Scale Questions (rate from 1 to 5, etc.):

- The course met my expectations.
- The course met my needs.
- I have information I can use on the job.
- The course was interesting.
- The course was enjoyable.
- The material was covered at just the right pace.
- The material was covered in the right depth.
- I would recommend this course to someone else.
- There was adequate opportunity for me to practice what I learned.

Short Answer Questions:

- The most valuable thing I learned was:
- One way to make the course better would be to:

Questions Unique to an e-Learning Course

In addition to the information above, you will also want to ask questions about the delivery method, the technology, and the ease of use. Questions might include:

Likert Scale Questions:

- The course was easy to use.
- The course had no technical problems.
- The course downloaded quickly.

Short Answer Questions:

- How would you describe your experience with the online format of this course?

Other Questions

Based on your particular programs, you may also want questions to assess the instructor or the registration and log on process if you are dealing with Webcasts or, perhaps, the ease of navigation to find and launch a course from the LMS.

Methods for Collecting Data

You might design a Level 1 evaluation for an e-learning course to automatically appear in the course at the end, to automatically launch when the user exits, or to be e-mailed to the user after the fact. It may be created and managed through your authoring tool, through your Learning Management System, or just through your e-mail system.

The challenge with a Level 1 evaluation in the e-learning world is getting your students to complete the survey. There is no instructor standing at the door asking everyone for the evaluation before they leave. Therefore, you may want to consider various follow-up methods or motivation strategies to encourage completion of the survey. For example:

- Make sure the survey pops up for the user, rather than just providing a link they must click.
- Send reminder e-mails to anyone who hasn't completed a survey.
- Require an evaluation to be filled out before a certificate can be issued.
- Provide a small gift or other token for anyone who completes the survey.
- Enter each person who completes the survey into a drawing for a prize.

Level 2 Evaluation: Learning

With a Level 2 evaluation, you are trying to determine if the students learned what they were supposed to learn. Did they meet the objectives?

Testing Within the Course

In most cases, the Level 2 evaluation is done with some sort of post-test that is part of the course. Testing was covered in detail in Chapter 7. You may choose to have only a post-test to determine the student's ending level of knowledge. Or, if appropriate, you might include a pre-test and a post-test so you can see the difference to know how much of their final knowledge is a result of the course itself.

Blended Approaches

Based on the course's objectives and the type of content, some of the Level 2 evaluation might be conducted in person. You may need the student to demonstrate a specific skill, speak about an attitude, or demonstrate a behavior in a real-world environment. In these situations, you might have an instructor or mentor moderate an assessment in order to determine the student's mastery of the objectives. For example, a medical technician course might teach the proper procedures and techniques for drawing blood. But when it comes time for the students to "graduate," they need to perform the procedure on a medical dummy with feedback from an instructor.

Validating Your Tests

In order for you to be able to trust the results of your Level 2 testing, your tests need to be well designed. During the design and development of the course, you'll want to make sure they adequately test the objectives, aren't too easy or too hard, are legally sound, and are fairly safeguarded against cheating.

Once the test has been developed and deployed, you may want to review overall scores per question. This can help identify possible problems with either the question or the content. If you find that most questions, on average, have about an 85% success rate but there is one question with a 35% success rate, you might have an issue. You can then review the question and the related content to try to rectify the situation. Possible causes include:

- The question was programmed incorrectly.
- The directions are unclear.
- The question is unclear.

- The question is misleading.
- The answers are too subjective.
- The related content was not covered adequately in the course (not covered at all, not covered in sufficient detail, not explained clearly, or not given enough emphasis).

Levels 3 – 5 Evaluation: Impact

In a corporate environment, you generally don't train just to train. You generally don't spend the time and effort to develop and deliver a course just for the sake of having the knowledge. You want to accomplish something! You probably have some sort of business goal; some sort of change you want to see. Evaluation Levels 3, 4, and 5 help you determine just what the impact of the training was.

Level 3: Transfer

A Level 3 evaluation helps you to determine whether or not students' behaviors actually change as a result of new learning. You'll want to find out if they are they doing what they are supposed to be doing, believing what they are supposed to be believing, etc.

A Level 3 evaluation is generally conducted 3 to 6 months after the training and is often done in the actual work environment. Some methods to find out if the skills, knowledge, or attitudes are being used by the learners include observations and surveys with supervisors, customers, or co-workers.

Examples of observation checklist items or survey questions include:

- Does the subject use protective eyewear when operating the machinery?
- Does the subject verify the identity of the customer before answering questions about an account?
- Does the subject ask for additional leads from the customer?

Level 4: Results

Before you embarked on this training initiative, someone believed that training would benefit the organization in some way. A Level 4 evaluation proves (or disproves) that belief. The students may have enjoyed the class, learned what they were supposed to learn, and used the information properly on the job. Those things alone, however, do not mean the business results will automatically be achieved.

The challenge with a Level 4 evaluation is that there are often many factors involved in a business issue. Even if the training is effective, another factor may have prevented the issue being resolved, improved, etc. Conversely, the training may have been ineffective while another factor was successful in resolving the issue. How do you know what training can take the credit (blame) for?

Unfortunately, there is no good answer to that question. You can, at least, do your best to measure the improvements desired. Refer back to your business case to see what you hoped to accomplish: increased sales, reduced complaints, reduced turnover, increased efficiency, increased production, fewer accidents, etc. Then you can gather data on these outcomes. You'll probably want to identify other factors that may have impacted the results as well.

Level 5: Return on Investment

Some training practitioners consider return on investment (ROI) to be a part of Level 4, while others consider it as its own level. Regardless of what level you put it in, you may want to attach dollar figures to your business results. Just as you looked at the potential ROI when you were deciding to embark on this endeavor (Chapter 2), you can use the same guidelines to calculate the actual ROI.

Summary

An e-learning project is a significant endeavor. A lot of time, money, and effort probably went into it, so it makes sense to stop and see if it was worth it. Unfortunately, many companies do not take these steps because they, too, will take up time, money, and effort. The best way to ensure that you are able to undertake an evaluation effort is to build it into your project plan from the very beginning.

12

Preparing Yourself for the Future

So far this book has walked you through the steps for taking your e-learning course from an idea to full-scale implementation. You have learned the process of conducting your needs analysis, designing your course, developing the different elements that will meet your objectives, implementing what you have created, and then evaluating your course. So, what now?

The future of e-learning continues to change as technology advances, as new ideas are implemented and tested, and as more and more companies implement e-learning initiatives. You will want to stay on top of the changes so you can grow with them.

This chapter outlines the skills you can develop to be effective (and marketable) as an e-learning professional as well as where you can go to get some of those skills.

Skills/Career Opportunities

There are multiple skills that can help you become a well-versed e-learning expert. In chapter 3, the specialized talents and roles you may need for your e-learning course were identified. These consist of:

- Instructional Designer
- Researcher
- Writer
- Proofreader
- Editor
- Programmer for Course Assembly
- Graphic Designer
- Quality Assurance Tester
- Project Manager
- Subject-Matter Expert
- Online Instructor
- Voice Talent
- Audio Recording and Editing Specialist
- Video Production and Editing Specialist

Since these talents and roles are valuable to have when working on an e-learning project, a good first step toward preparing for the future is to gain new skills that would help you fill these roles. You could also look at this list as a primer on careers in e-learning.

Instructional Design

Chapters 5, 6, and 7 outlined the questions you need to ask and decisions that need to be made when you are designing an e-learning course. Knowing what elements should be included in the course, meeting the needs of the requirements document, making the content meet the objectives, and making sure your course is instructionally sound is the job of the instructional designer.

Writing/Course Developing

The writer takes the information gathered from subject-matter experts or source materials and writes the course content based on the guidelines in the design document. On some projects, the writer simply presents the teaching content and then an instructional designer adds the special instructional elements such as questions, interactions, etc. On some projects, the writer does that part as well. The writer (sometimes referred to as the course developer) writes storyboards, scripts any audio or video narrative, and includes special instructions to programmers about how the course should work.

Editing

The ability to edit your own work, as well as someone else's, is a valued skill to have for any project. For an e-learning project, editing up-front is extremely important because making changes after a course has already been programmed is expensive. In addition, e-learning courses are generally more text intensive than instructor-led courses.

The skills you may want to develop could vary based on the project or based on your role. There are three levels to editing:

- Proofreading – A proofreader would look for errors in spelling and grammar, style issues and adherence to project standards and guidelines.

- Editing – An editor looks for the same errors as a proofreader, but also offers suggestions on how to improve the writing and the content.

- Instructional design editing – An instructional design editor will look for the same errors as an editor, but also looks for instructional design flaws and how to make it better *training*. For example, an instructional design editor would make sure that the questions adequately match the objectives.

Programming/Course Assembly

The skills you would want to have to program your courses will depend on the tool you choose. Chapter 4 discussed the possible tools of the e-learning trade. Some tools require only a simple knowledge of Windows-based software. If you are proficient in Microsoft **Word** or **PowerPoint**, then you will be ready to go. Other tools require specialized knowledge of scripting language or of advanced features within that particular tool. Often, formal training is the best way to build these skills.

Graphic Design

A graphic designer is someone skilled in visualizing and creating the visual elements of a course, from the interface design to custom-developed graphics to involved interactions. There are three types of graphic designs skills you could work to master:

- Editing already created still graphics – you may want to change various elements of an existing graphic, such as its color. The ability to edit an existing graphic can be helpful if you are working with screenshots from a live software application and need to alter the data so confidential information is not displayed in your course.

- Custom still graphics – you may want to create a custom still graphics, such as a diagram, to enhance your content.

- 3-D or animated graphics – you may want to create 3-D or motion graphics for things you can't videotape. For example, it is not possible to videotape how a heart beats, but a 3-D image can show how the hear pump and how the blood flows through the ventricles.

3-D or animated graphics are the most expensive to outsource, and is also a skill that is more difficult to learn than working with still graphics. However, you may choose to develop this skill so you can create these custom graphics that you may not have the budget for.

Quality Assurance Testing

In chapter 11 you learned what it takes to test your course for quality. The quality assurance tester needs to be able to try to "break" the course. It is the job of the tester to go through each screen and make sure each button and interaction is working properly. This person needs to have attention to detail and troubleshooting skills.

Online Instructing

The online instructor teaches a synchronous course through a webcast or other online application. Online instructors will want to have the following skills:

- An understanding of the technology. Most of the webcast products have the same offerings as the others. You may find some differences, but you probably will need the ability to show presentation slides, use marking tools to point to areas on your slides, share your desktop, and collect written, visual, and verbal feedback from the learners.

- The ability to multitask. The online instructor has to be able to teach the class, read and process feedback from learners, and navigate the webcasting application. Some instructors have assistants who respond to questions that the learners type to the instructor to help minimize the need for multitasking.

- A good, clear speaking voice. If the students can only hear your voice, you will need to make sure you are able to be understood and that your voice carries interest and enthusiasm.

- The ability to teach to a camera. If your webcasting courseware allows videostreaming, you will want to become comfortable training in front of a video camera. You will want to look as natural in front of the camera as you do in front of a classroom. A course in television journalism can help you go a long way toward becoming a talented online instructor.

Voice/Video Talent

As with the online trainer, a course in television journalism or radio might be a good start toward developing this talent. Voice and video talent are often contracted out to professionals in the field.

Audio Recording and Editing

The ability to record and edit audio is becoming easier due to user-friendly technology. The days of recording on audio tape is gone and digital production is the norm. Most computers are sold with **Windows Movie Maker** which makes audio recording a snap. All you need for a good audio recording is a quality microphone and someone with a good, clear speaking voice.

Video Production and Editing

The skills needed to produce and edit quality video is a bit more complex than simply having **Windows Movie Maker**. You need to have either a quality digital camera or the hardware to convert analog tape to digital – and learn how to use it. Even with these aids, you may have a need for additional specialized knowledge and equipment to get a good picture and quality audio, as well as the editing work that follows.

Resources to Help Learn More

Websites

Electronic sources (websites, e-newsletters, etc.) are often the best choices for learning more about e-learning. Because the field and the technology are changing so rapidly, you need current information – and these resources are generally more current than books that have a long lead time or conferences that plan their sessions almost a year in advance. Website offerings may include:

- Articles
- Bibliographies
- Blogs
- Calculators
- Conference calendars
- Demonstrations
- Discussion boards
- e-Newsletters
- Forums
- Links to other sites
- Newsletters
- Podcasts
- Products
- Reviews
- Sample courses
- Templates
- Videos
- Webinar offerings
- White papers

Figure 12.1 Website Resources

Go to the Resources page at **www.e-LearningUncovered.com** for a downloadable version of these resources with links.

Website	Description
ASTD: Learning Circuits http://www.learningcircuits.org	Contains links, articles, and headlines for the e-learning industry.
Brandon-Hall http://www.brandon-hall.com	Contains information about technology trends, tools, vendors, and best practices.
e-Learning Centre http://www.e-learningcentre.co.uk	Contains links to e-learning articles, books, products and services, conferences, and examples of best practices.
e-Learning Guru http://www.e-learningguru.com	Contains how-to articles, templates, and calculators in the tool box, white papers, book summaries, and links.
eLearning News http://www.elearningnews.net	Contains news, reviews, and information posted by other e-learning professionals.
eLearningPost http://www.elearningpost.com/articles/	Contains news, views, and stories around such things as Corporate Learning and Instructional Design.
e-Learning Resources for Trainers http://www.susan-boyd.com/online-training-resources.htm	Contains information to help trainers find out about the e-learning products and services that are available.
e-Learning Resources http://www.grayharriman.com/	Gives information on e-learning, online learning, distance learning, blended learning, adult learning, and related resources.
eLearnspace http://www.elearnspace.org	Contains information to help you explore e-learning networks and technology.
Learning Circuits http://www.astd.org/LC/	Provides current and archived *Learning Circuit* articles.
Masie Center http://www.masie.com	Contains e-learning resources, including the free digital book, *701 e-Learning Tips.*
mLearning hub http://www.mlearninghub.com/	Contains news, technology information, blogs, and other resources for mobile learning.
The eLearning Guild http://www.elearningguild.com	Serves as a global community for designers, developers, and managers of e-learning.
Training Magazine http://www.trainingmag.com	Provides publications and resources for developments in training and online learning tools and techniques.

Books

e-Learning books can be great reference tools, as long as they are current. They allow you to go into much more depth than online articles or newsletters.

Since many e-learning books can't be purchased through your local bookstore, it is often impossible to look at a book before you buy it. If you can, look at the table of contents to see if the book will meet your needs.

Figure 12.2 Book Resources

Go to the Resources page at **www.e-LearningUncovered.com** for a downloadable version of these resources with links.

Website	Description
Amazon.com http://www.amazon.com/	A search for "e-learning" reveals over 1000 results.
ASTD e-Learning Handbook http://books.mcgraw-hill.com/ authors/rossett/	A handbook developed by ASTD to explain what training professionals need to know about e-Learning.
e-Learning Bibliography http://elisa.ugm.ac.id/page_view.php?Bimbingan_KMPK&57	Provides a "bibliography" type document with 23 e-learning books.
e-Learning Centre http://www.e-learningcentre.co.uk/ Bookshop/books.htm	Lists books in association with Amazon.
eLearning Guild http://www.elearningguild.com/content.cfm?selection=doc.545	Gives several free e-books.
e-LearningHub.com http://www.e-learninghub.com/books/	Lists some of the "more popular" e-learning books.
e-Learning Site http://www.e-learningsite.com/ links/books.htm	Recommends e-learning books.

Conferences

To get information in e-learning, you can attend certain sessions in a standard training conference or go to one dedicated to e-learning. You will want to check the program brochure to see what each conference offers.

Conferences provide two outlets for learning. The sessions are tailored to meet learning objectives, and the expo hall gives information on technology trends and vendor options. Some conferences also offer a third outlet and deliver some of their sessions online through podcasts or Webinars.

Figure 12.3 Conference Resources

Go to the Resources page at **www.e-LearningUncovered.com** for a downloadable version of these resources with links.

Website	Description
American Society for Training and Development (ASTD) http://www.astd.org/content/conferences/	Lists the upcoming conferences brought to you by ASTD.
Conference Alerts http://www.conferencealerts.com/elearning.htm	Lists e-learning conferences worldwide.
e-Learning Centre http://www.e-learningcentre.co.uk/eclipse/conferences/index.html	Lists e-learning conferences worldwide.
eLearning Guild http://www.elearningguild.com/pbuild/linkbuilder.cfm?selection=fol.7	Lists the upcoming conferences brought to you by the eLearning Guild.
Elearning! Summit http://events.unisfair.com/index.jsp?eid=437&seid=29	Gives information on virtual events with educational sessions, an exhibit hall, and networking opportunities.
Training Magazine www.trainingmagevents.com	Lists the upcoming conferences brought to you by Training Magazine.

Certifications

When you are looking to expand your knowledge on e-learning, you have three options for expanding your knowledge.

- Go to the school of hard knocks.
- Get certification(s).
- Get a degree in e-learning.

Each of these three choices can give you valuable skills, and any could be the right choice for you depending on your personal learning goals. Certifications, however, often give you the quickest results. For example, a certificate could be earned in days, weeks, or months (depending on the program), where other options could take years to get you to your goal.

Figure 12.4 Certification Resources

Go to the Resources page at **www.e-LearningUncovered.com** for a downloadable version of these resources with links.

Website	Description
ASTD http://www.astd.org/content/education/certificatePrograms/certificates-workshops.htm	Gives links to several e-learning certificates available online.
CyberU http://www.cyberu.com/home.asp	Contains links to many certificate programs, not just e-learning.
Distance Education Clearinghouse http://www.uwex.edu/disted/certificates.cfm	Lists 20 certificate programs.
e-Learners.com http://www.elearners.com/index.asp	Contains links to many certificate programs, including e-learning.
e-Learning Center http://www.e-learningcenter.com/	Gives links to certifications courses for e-learning development.
Langevin Learning Services www.langevinonline.com	Lists many workshops for certification.
Learning Times http://www.learningtimes.net/certified.shtml	Offers e-learning certifications.
World Wide Learn http://www.worldwidelearn.com/	Offers links to many certification programs, including e-learning.

e-Newsletters

e-Newsletters are generally distributed through e-mail and are good resources to keep you current with the trends in e-learning. These newsletters often give information about new technologies and answers to problems that face others in the e-learning field.

Figure 12.5 Newsletter Resources

Go to the Resources page at **www.e-LearningUncovered.com** for a downloadable version of these resources with links.

Website	Description
Bersin & Associates http://www.bersin.com/News/ NewsletterEl.aspx?id=330	Provides monthly newsletters, including e-learning.
eLearners.com http://www.elearners.com/ resources/index.asp	Provides a weekly e-mail newsletter on news, trends, resources and organizations that impact the e-learning marketplace.
eLearning Awards 2004 http://elearningawards.eun.org/ww/en/ pub/elearningawards2004/news/news1.htm	An archive of newsletter award winners. Original documents are in the languages they were written, and many are in English.
eLearningPost http://www.elearningpost.com/	A digest of feature articles and daily links to articles and news stories about corporate learning.
Training Magazine http://www.trainingmag.com/msg/ newsletter/training/index.jsp?	Provides three monthly e-learning newsletters.

Blogs

Since a blog is a Web log, you can get valuable information from others in the e-learning field. The blog is comprised of text, hypertext, images, and links. You can subscribe to them; and many show comments from other readers. Because they are often on different topics shown in reverse chronological order, you will want to scroll through the entries to see which blogs interest you. If you want to learn more about what a blog is, here is a great blog about blogs: http://www.problogger.net/archives/2006/02/14/what-is-a-blog-2/

Figure 12.6 Blog Resources

Go to the Resources page at **www.e-LearningUncovered.com** for a downloadable version of these resources with links.

Website	Description
eLearning Technology http://elearningtech.blogspot.com/	Blog on e-learning technology, such as trends, Web 2.0, and tools.
elearningpost.com http://www.elearningpost.com/	Explores news, views, and stories around Corporate Learning, Community Building, Instructional Design, Knowledge Management and more.
Learning on the Leading Edge http://www.bersin.com/Blog/BlogList.aspx	Explores learning solutions and technology including tools, LMSs, social networking, content management, and learning 2.0.
Online Learning News and Research http://people.uis.edu/rschr1/onlinelearning/blogger.html	Explores e-learning with a focus on academia.
The Learning Circuits Blog (ASTD) http://learningcircuits.blogspot.com/	A community feature of Learning Circuits dedicated to sharing ideas and opinions about the state of learning and technology.
The Rapid e-Learning Blog http://www.articulate.com/rapid-elearning/	Shares practical tips and tricks on rapid e-learning.

Forums

Forums, or discussion boards, give opportunities for e-learning professionals to share information. They give you the opportunity to ask questions, give advice, see what the trends are, get opinions on current technology, and even see what other professionals are doing with their courses. Often, they allow you to learn from others' mistakes and get information on what has worked (or hasn't worked) for them.

Figure 12.7 Forum Resources

Go to the Resources page at **www.e-LearningUncovered.com** for a downloadable version of these resources with links.

Website	Description
ASQ Discussion Boards http://www.asq.org/discussionBoards/forum.jspa?forumID=49	Provides online discussion boards for various topics. e-Learning is discussed on the boards for this link.
ASTD http://community.astd.org/eve/ubb.x?a=frm&s=4201061&f=6401041	Provides online forums. All are on training and many are e-learning specific.
e-Learning Centre http://www.e-learningcentre.co.uk/eclipse/vendors/discussion.htm	Provides discussion boards and forum tools.

Summary

As you prepare for the future, keep your sights on what is possible for e-learning. The e-learning field has grown leaps and bounds over the past few years. With this growth comes a need for e-learning professionals to stay current with the e-learning technology, hone current skills, and add new ones.

Glossary

ADDIE Model	The training development model that uses the following steps: Analyze, Design, Develop, Implement, and Evaluate.
Alt-text	The small pop-up that describes the graphic when you put your mouse over a graphic on a web document.
Animations	Moving graphics (which might simulate the flow through a production process, for example).
Application Sharing	A feature of a webcast that gives the presenter the ability to share desktops with students.
ASP Software	Software, hosted by a vendor. You pay for access to it for a set period of time.
Asynchronous Learning	Learning that occurs when the instructor and students do not participate at the same time.
Blended Learning	Using two or more learning formats to help meet your objectives, such as combining e-learning and classroom learning.
Bookmark	Bookmarks allow the student to come back to the point where they last left off.
Blog	Short for Web log, a type of Website where someone writes short entries on a regular basis, much like a column in a newspaper.
CAL	An e-learning acronym that stands for Computer-Assisted Learning.

Caveat Emptor	Let the buyer beware.
CBT	An e-learning acronym that stands for Computer Based Training.
Chat	A feature of a webcast where participants can send a message to the instructor to make a comment or ask a question.
CMI	An e-learning acronym that stands for Computer-Managed Instruction.
Collaboration	The activity of learners working together to reach a learning goal.
Computer-Based Training (CBT)	Any e-learning course designed to be housed on the World Wide Web, an intranet, or a computer disk.
Computer Simulations	On-screen demonstrations of how the software works.
Cost Benefit Ratio	A calculation method that allows you to present your bottom line numbers and uses the following formula: Financial Benefits ÷ Total Cost of Training = Cost Benefit Ratio.
Course Authoring Tools	Electronic tools used to assemble e-learning courseware.
Course Element Tools	Specialized software that can be used during e-learning development for elements, such as graphics software, software simulation, and assessment tools.
Design Document	A document that includes information about the decisions you made including objectives and instructional design strategies.
Development Ratios	The estimated ratio of time to develop a course verses the course seat time.
Disincentives	Anything that may make someone *not* want to take a course.
e-Learning	A course or structured learning event that uses an electronic medium to meet its objectives.
Embedded Questions	Questions sprinkled throughout the content of the course.

End-User Testing	Testing the course with the end-user to make sure they understand, enjoy, and learn from the course what they need to learn.
Forum	A collaborative learning experience where questions or comments are posted along with a trail of responses that are posted and archived regarding the original message.
Graphics	Media that includes still photography, clip art pictures, graphs, or diagrams.
Hosted Software	Software, hosted by a vendor. You pay for access to the software for a set period of time.
HRIS	Human Resource Information System
HTML Editor	A software package that allows you to build HTML pages either by creating the code yourself or by designing the pages visually and allowing the software to create the code behind-the-scenes for you.
Human Resource Information System (HRIS)	A system that tracks Human Resource related employee data such as personal information, salaries, performance, and payroll.
Incentives	Anything that may make someone want to take a course.
Integration Testing	Testing the course to assure it operates properly with any other related systems, such as a Learning Management System.
Interactions	A back-and-forth exchange between the student and the e-learning course, such as questions, activities, and games.
Interface	The electronic framework that is between the student and the courseware.
IT	Information Technology Department
LCMS	Learning Content Management System
Learning Content Management System	A management system used to help developers who reuse much of the content between courses organize and store their content.

Glossary

Learning Management System (LMS)
A system that can either simply track completion of individual courses, or it can manage the learning and development of the entire organization.

LMS
Learning Management System

Load Testing
Testing the course to assure it, and the systems that support it, operate properly when used by the projected number of people.

Media
The audio, video, graphic, or animation elements on an e-learning course.

Message Board
A collaborative learning experience where questions or comments are posted and a trail of responses are posted and archived regarding the original message.

Metadata
In reference to Reusable Learning Objects, this is data about the data.

m-Learning
A course or structured learning event that focuses on learning through a mobile device, such as a cell phone.

Naming Conventions
How the module documents and files are named for retrieval.

Navigation
How the student accesses the information and moves within the interface of an e-learning course.

Object Repositories
In reference to Reusable Learning Objects, this is a place to store and catalog the objects so they can be found and re-used.

Objective
A learning goal for the course.

Off-the-Shelf Courseware
e-Learning courseware that can be purchased from a vendor that can be used without needing custom development.

Packaged Software
Software that you purchase, install, and can use as much as you want to.

PowerPoint Conversion Tool
A tool that will allow you to turn a PowerPoint file into an e-learning course.

Project Plan
The plan containing the details that will tell how you will make your strategic plan happen.

Prototype	A small section of a course that helps you make sure the assumptions and decisions you made during the design phase are valid and translate well when they move from the drawing board to actual production.
QA	Quality assurance
Randomization	Mixing up the order of the questions or using different questions each time.
Rapid Development	The process of developing e-learning faster, without sacrificing quality.
RCO	Reusable Content Object
Remediation	Any feedback given to a student during a practice or test exercise.
Return on Investment (ROI)	A calculation method that allows you to present your bottom line numbers and uses the following formula: (Total Benefits − Total Costs) ÷ Total Costs × 100 = ROI
Reusable Learning Object (RLO)	A chunk of electronic content that can be accessed individually that completely accomplishes a single learning goal and can prove it.
RFI	Request for Information
RFP	Request for Proposal
RIO	Reusable Information Object
RLO	Reusable Learning Object
ROI	Return on Investment
SCO	Sharable Courseware Object
SCORM/AICC	Sharable Courseware Object Reference Model / Aviation Industry CBT Committee. Interoperability standards that ensure e-learning products work together.
Section 508	A federal law for accessibility of electronic communications to people with disabilities.
SME	Subject Matter Expert
Social Media	Media designed to be disseminated through social interaction using tools such as wikis, blogs, and social networking sites such as Facebook and LinkedIn.

Storyboard	The blueprint of your course.
Strategic Plan	A plan that explains what you are trying to do, why you are trying to do it, and how you are going to get there.
Synchronous Learning	Learning that occurs when an instructor and students are together at the same time – but not necessarily in the same physical place.
TBT	An e-learning acronym that stands for Technology-Based Training.
Threaded Discussion	A collaborative learning experience where questions or comments are posted and a trail of responses are posted and archived regarding the original message.
TMS	Training Management System
Training Management System (TMS)	A term that can be defined as one of two things: 1. A system that tracks only classroom training, or 2. A system that tracks e-learning completion, but not other learning functions.
Virtual Classroom Learning	Learning that combines elements of the synchronous and asynchronous world. There are students and an instructor as well as a specified beginning and end date; however, within the course, students learn and communicate at their own pace.
WBT	An e-learning acronym that stands for Web-Based Training.
Web-Based Training (WBT)	An e-learning course, designed to be housed on the World Wide Web, that is taken while you are connected to the Internet.
Webcast	A synchronous course that is presented over the World Wide Web.
Whiteboards	A feature of a webcast that lets the presenter make marks on any of the slides or blank screens.
Wiki	A type of Website that uses a special software allowing easy creation and editing of interlinked Web pages.
Workstation Testing	Testing the course to assure it will run properly on the various configurations of the workstations in the organization.

Index

Be sure to visit
www.e-LearningUncovered.com
for more great tips and
resources!

Other books in
the E-Learning
Uncovered Series

**E-Learning Uncovered:
Lectora Publisher 2009**

**E-Learning Uncovered:
Articulate Studio 2009**

Available Fall 2009

Made in the USA
Lexington, KY
22 February 2011